# Carrying the Chalice Forward

# Carrying the Chalice Forward

# CARRYING THE CHALICE FORWARD

## And Other Secret Stories of North America

BY

MARTIN CARRIERE

Great White Eagle
Kischi Wapa Keliwa

**Bois Brule/Metis**

Arranged by
Stanley J. St. Clair

# Carrying the Chalice Forward

© 2010 Martin Carriere
St. Clair Publications

All rights reserved. No part of this publication may be reproduced or transmitted in any form by any means electronic or mechanical, including telecopy, recording, or any information storage and retrieval system now known or invented, without permission in writing from the publisher, except by a reviewer who wishes to quote brief passages in connection with a review written for inclusion in a magazine, newspaper or broadcast.

Published in the United States of America

ISBN 978-1-935786-09-2

St. Clair Publications
P. O. Box 726
Mc Minnville, TN 37110-0726, USA
**http://stan.stclair.net**

# Carrying the Chalice Forward

## *Contents*

| | |
|---|---|
| Acknowledgements | 7 |
| 1 –Spirit Journey | 11 |
| 2 –Committed | 27 |
| 3 –Songs of Culture and Eternity | 31 |
| 4 –In the Beginning | 51 |
| 5 –In the Houses of the Holy Blood | 73 |
| 6. –Four Astride a Horse | 77 |
| 7 –Pharaoh's Dream | 87 |
| 8 –Letting Go of Paradise | 97 |
| 9 –Carrying the Chalice Forward | 105 |
| 10 –United Families | 147 |
| 11 –Feudal Rule in the Americas | 165 |
| Biographical Sketch of the Author | 178 |

# Carrying the Chalice Forward

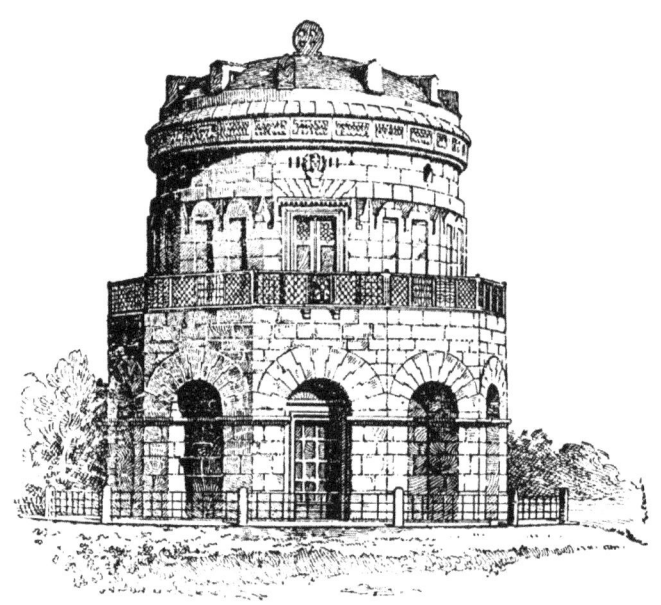

# *Acknowledgements*

We wish to acknowledge first our princely gentleman cousin, Stanley St. Clair, for his encouragement and forthrightness of heart in helping bring this publication to fulfillment. We are forever grateful for our elders, visionaries and our children for reaching out with their long arms and opening the doors to our souls. We wish to thank our numerous French Canadian and Celtic cousins who thrill at the joy of finding their indigenous connections and origins. Words cannot cover the undying thanks we owe for the amount of material unearthed by many Metis researchers and family searching to learn the truth. Thanks to the true brotherhoods of men and women for their encouragement and for creating symbols like the fleur-de-lis, the tree of life and the word "perseverance" for us to follow on our journeys through so many otherwise closed doors. A special thanks to the mammoth efforts of timeless scions like Niven Sinclair for encouraging our families to step forward with our strengths and our stories to help correct the miswritten histories of the New World.

We wish to praise the lifelong efforts of timeless Metis examples of courage and devotion to uncovering the truth of our family by Dr. John Roberts, Paul Chaput, Dr. Devine, Dr. Campbell, my friend Darren, and many,

# Carrying the Chalice Forward

many others. Very special thanks also to our old antiquarian friend and devotee of the Stone of Destiny, Dr. Hugh MacMillan, without whose lifelong efforts many of the histories of our families would be lost. Besides the natural encouragement of my mother, I wish to thank the rest of our family for standing in for me when I was too busy to do my own chores.

Many of our family walk the quiet road and selflessly help the truth of our understandings, of living with good conscience, to fill with grace each step we make. One such soldier was Richard Coleman who most recently left our collective life journey to watch us from afar. This following song of family tribute is written in his honour.

## *WALKING THE DREAM*

Standing tall as a prince amoung men
Brotherly, soft spoken; a good friend
Loving gentle kindness in every step
The truth of love in his eyes watching
As his hearts desire journeys near and far
Walking together this sweet community
Bearing the truth so that all may hear
That princes did walk and journeyed here
As brother to brothers and true friend dear
Who now stands taller and richer still
For in his absence our journey is clear
To stand tall with eyes watching
For our loved ones far and near

# Carrying the Chalice Forward

Dreaming of family and endless years
Where from under rock and carrying a stride
We walk together with mountainous pride
Gently holding dear our loved ones near
And ever searching here for time to stay
And hear the tales of journeys far
That brought us all back under the same star

We wish to offer special thanks to our cousin, William Mann, for writing such entertaining books of our early settlements and to other family like Steve St. Clair, Mark Staveley; also Susan English, D'Elayne Coleman, Elizabeth Lane and other Atlantic Conference supporters for their unwavering efforts to keep the actions of our family moving forward. A special thanks to our extended Carriere family in Windsor for the volumes of helpful research material and excerpts. Extreme gratefulness to our Algonquin, Chippewa, Nipissing, six nations and other cousins and all of the remainder of our family and allies stepping forward as part of the conscious awakening of the new-world of conscience and goodwill.

A brotherhood of appreciation to Chief J. Geissel and his loving partner Sue for their diligent and ongoing commitment towards expanding the early records of our mutual families. We offer our sincere acknowledgements for our Cree and Soto cousins of the old families out west in Saskatchewan for

# Carrying the Chalice Forward

sharing their Midewiwin and traditional understandings of things.

Thanks also to my son, Benjamin, for his continuing patience at sitting through so many hours, weeks and months of discussions and talking; and for allowing us the time and space to continue the writing of our family's story.

# 1

## *Spirit Journey*

# Carrying the Chalice Forward

# 1

## *Spirit Journey*

*Our teachings have always been that the heart, (the love based seat of the soul), in balance with the collective soul of all creation; knows best what it is we need to hear.*

*Lost in the twists and turns of history, the soul of the world still cries to be heard and speaks to us in our dreams of our responsibilities. In our visions and our sight we are each given the knowledge that all of our actions on this earth and in our hearts are our own individual contribution to the health of the world. The collective soul of this planet relies on our internal connections to the Creator, and our being awakens to our true paths and journeys within creation; so that our outward expressions are in line with the great purpose of our souls. Our acceptance of the dream allows the heart of creation to act as our guiding force to create a truly beautiful world and enter the truth of our own souls.*

*It seems that the forces of procreation and survival, or play and duty, shall always co-exist in this duo-cosmic creation we call civilization. How we work with, or play with, each of these forces is our uniquely individual decision. What we ultimately gain through our joining with the collective soul,*

# Carrying the Chalice Forward

*through dream and shared vision with the rest of creation; while being pulled by the forces of play and duty, is what forms the flower of our true human expression as we each step forth from this muddy, befuddling ooze we call creation. The level of understanding we each attain through this process can only be measured by how easy it is for us to laugh at our own predicaments.*

*The understanding is that to live our own lives fully we can only hold to love and the honouring of our own soul's journey. In this way, our only true hope is to forever remain in balance with this beautiful co-expression of life we call creation. Selfless caring for the earth, air, wind and forces of union, that fill our void with wonder, stretches us beyond the slave-like obedience demanded by our sometimes subservient parents and administrators. When the journey becomes the high priority we lift ourselves beyond the subjection of our spirits and reach into the divine inspiration that brings forth life and love.*

*For those who have journeyed to this land it is good to remember that our teachings, as handed down and remembered, from teachers like Odin, Jeshua, Deganawideh and others are: for us each to become whole hearted wherever we live and to embody the land where we reside with the full beauty of our spirit. Our hope is that when we come to love the land and nurture it as our shared gift to our peacefully enjoined children our civilized heart and soul will emerge – until then we remain uncivilized and unwelcomed by the land and the true people of*

## Carrying the Chalice Forward

*the land. By remembering the truth of the joining of our children we honour the process and can freely then rejoice in the grand mystery of life.*

### Spirit Journey

The soul is an empty valley only the forgotten dare to enter
The soul is an empty valley only the forgotten dare to enter
The soul is an empty valley only the forgotten dare to enter
The soul...

As I repeated these words in my mind...

As I walked, all last night, along the edge of the broken path of this little island; my heart has been troubled and unsure. I strolled aimlessly along the stone block path. A wide border of stone edged the path sloping down to the surface of a deep green pool slowly rising and falling with the tide. Above the water, rocks were covered in layers of moss, dead seaweed and snails. Below, the rocks were covered in a dark green sludge that swayed with the motion of the water.

This was a secluded part of the ocean hemmed in by a man-made island. A haven for artists and writers like me: A place to wander and not be seen; a place to speak and always be heard.

# Carrying the Chalice Forward

All night I have felt a deep emptiness in the core of my stomach.

A body was found last night.

As I stood on the edge of the wooden pier looking over the mirrored stillness of the water I rested my arms on the heavy wooden board railing watching the spot where the dead Indian was pulled from the water. Some said he was murdered; others said he was drunk and stumbled into the water; a few thought he may have been fishing and fell out of his boat. But I knew this was my friend, Joe Two Rivers, who was now free of his anger and his shame at not being able to adjust to, or conquer, the Whiteman's ways.

I wondered peacefully to myself: *What would happen if Joe's spirit (as I had dreamed all last night) really lived within me now? How would it change me? Would I now be considered Indian? Would I suffer and die and never satisfy my spirit? Would I forever be alone and outside the Whiteman's world? A stranger in my own land? Surely, Whitemen only judge an Indian by the colour of his skin? Or is the soul of the Indian outcast as well?* A wave of sorrow flowed over me for the loss of my friend as I strove to understand the questions death brought to my mind.

The heavy weight of sorrow surged in my chest, bringing tears to my eyes. I felt a tear drop slowly to my exposed hand and roll on to

# Carrying the Chalice Forward

the wooden beam and slide down into the water.

I felt weary and heavy—the spirit of Joe Two Rivers fresh in my mind. A wavering image with deep furrows surrounding his friendly auburn eyes speaking of the myriad of emotion ready to jump to the surface—hidden only by wrinkles and the darkness of age. His forehead parted with a slick of black hair, like wet seaweed. His nose: large and pitted from many brawls, forced on him in youth and in bars. High cheeks and a firm jawbone supporting his countenance with dignity and respect. The long dark mane of hair at his back hung low below his waist, hiding the top of a pair of worn and faded jeans. A red and black lumberjack shirt draped over his shoulders.

*Joe Two Rivers: born and dead—now gone, lives somehow in my heart,* I thought as I moved back from the edge of the rail, releasing a deep sigh, feeling the heaviness of grief lower my eyelids and warm my cheeks with a flood that wouldn't ever stop flowing—flowing down into my soul to fill a hole that would not fill: an emptiness—nothing. A part of my body that was not there yet was felt with the intensity of an ocean storm. Part of the emptiness that existed before the world came to be.

I became very, very tired.

# Carrying the Chalice Forward

These same questions came into my mind over and over again: *What would I do if it rains? Would I not go out any longer than needed and not get fully wet? Or would I brave the chill and flailing of the wind and stay forever? Could I survive the wet? How could I protect my heart from the bitterness of the oppression?*

The confusion and chaos of the wind is easily seen as it strokes the top of the ocean inlet: criss-crossing, swirling, jumping, diving, turning; leaving an illegible jumble of furrows and waves undulating, changing, swerving, colliding, mixing—an unchangeable world of derision where the rules are made as the events occur and turmoil reigns supreme. Yet, below the surface, life goes on and the wind has no force to bend or change the rhythm of the deep: where the rain is lost in a myriad of molecules used and exhausted as a source of life—always: growing, developing, changing, dying; preserving life and death forever as one.

The slow unending reserve of time outlasts and passes under the fast-changing fragile world of dirt and reflections. For, what is the ocean but the depths of time and the beginning of life? Aren't all things on this earth covered with a wall of vapour hundreds of feet thick? We all seem to live in varying degrees of ocean. The fish in the depths are really just flying in a solid pool of vapour; and the residents of the land limited to hard ground and thin air:

## Carrying the Chalice Forward

constantly living and dying, changing and moving—living eternal reality: the regeneration of life. We are all one—we are all spirit. We live in an ocean of air with change and chaos reflected all around, yet we maintain an inner security of calm as a protection from time and erosion. Life will always go on and death will always be our brother.

As I stirred lightly in my half sleep, the image of Joe Two Rivers filled my mind with turmoil and a dark green haze—symbolic of life. Joe lifted both arms forming a semi-circle filled with light and began to change into a bird with golden wings and a bright red beak. He became covered in grey-black feathers with spots of orange on his chest. He flew upwards, rising steadily higher and higher. This bird called down to me from a long way up, inviting me on this journey. I began to lift from my sleep and to shrink into the smaller and smaller shape of a bird. I felt the emptiness in my stomach as a great force of gravity drawing me into the depths of nothingness and extinction. I opened my eyes and looked: for arms I now had wings like those of an eagle covered in light blue feathers; I now had a golden beak, and claws instead of feet. I rose steadily upwards past the clouds, the moon, and the stars—to the edge of the universe. There we slowed and stopped before a mysterious and wonderful ring of bright

# Carrying the Chalice Forward

golden feathers, ever turning, guarding the pathway to the distance beyond.

Joe signalled me not to speak to anyone except the very old man who handed out medicines, and greeted all newcomers — and not to join in any activities until the Great Spirit had arrived.

As Joe finished these warnings he flew through the golden ring of feathers into the spirit world. With caution, I followed after. Quickly we were surrounded by hundreds of birds of all different sizes and shapes, with feathers the colours of many rainbows. The birds hopped and danced all around with the joy of greeting two new arrivals. Joe returned their affectionate cries, and guided me quickly to the spot where the Old Medicine Man always stood waiting for new visitors to arrive.

I was suddenly overcome with the nausea that now I was no longer to have a part with the living, that this was my eternal home; without the touch of flesh or caress of the wind. The Old Medicine Man appeared before me and brought my mind to the realization that this was not my home until I had been accepted by the Great Spirit. I was overwhelmed by a sense of awe that such a place existed and that the Great Spirit would soon arrive. My awe turned to fear as I noticed that I alone had just one colour of feathers. My fear merged into wonder as all the residents of the spirit world

# Carrying the Chalice Forward

rose and circled in anticipation of the events about to unfold when the Great Spirit finally arrived.

A wave of song rushed into the air as I watched moving before me a dark cloud of night, tinged with red; in the centre of the pitchy black, blue effervescent rays streamed outward, fraying into tiny light beams of gold at the farthest edges. A bird like all the other birds began to take shape out of the darkness and seemed to absorb all of the darkness into its chest. The cloud of darkness disappeared into the chest of this little bird. No matter where I tried to look the tight explosive circle of night was always visible in the chest of this little bird.

The spirit world had risen in expectation of the arrival of the Great Spirit. All the animals and spirits stood silent—even their breath rolled into the hills of silence. The Great Spirit motioned for all the birds, animals, people and trees to gather in a circle all around so as to take part in a great mystery saved for this moment. I turned my head to try to see the edge of the circle and could not. All of my vision was filled with every manner of bird, animal and living thing—amoung which stood the largest forest ever seen and a sea that had no end. Lost in the tremendous power of my vision, I sank down on my claws and laid my head onto my outstretched wing—hoping for

## Carrying the Chalice Forward

oblivion—to wipe away my fear and lack of understanding and preparation for this event. The Great Spirit lifted a wing and a wave of silence spread out over the field of dreams. The wave smothered the voice that welled up inside me as my last plea of hope to escape before the Great Spirit spoke and sealed me into this world—where I had no brother and no home.

The beak of the Great Spirit opened and a loud rushing wind, with the force of many whales gathered close together, began to spin and circle around this large island of dreams. It waited hovering near the corridor of feathers—waiting to lead the spirits throughout the universe and to return with a host of gifts and presents for the Great Spirit. The Great Spirit sang to the wind a secret song—and as the time was not yet, the wind curled up into a spinning column of constantly moving images (taller than any totems or trees from the land of my birth). The song floated outward until it passed the edges of the world of dreams spreading to engulf the whole universe with its beauty and sorrow. The events this song foretold filled all the spirits with joy and with a longing for the end of this time and for the fulfillment of these wonderful things.

The song over, I slowly lifted my head from my wing and watched as all things faded from view except for the Great Spirit and me. Joe

## Carrying the Chalice Forward

and the Medicine Man were no longer visible. The only sign of motion was the golden ring of feathers: constantly turning, revolving. The darkness in the Great Spirit's chest began to expand: to grow, to fill the whole valley—the whole island, with darkness. An ancient cry of death rang loudly through the darkness as my spirit was pulled into the void, the centre of nothingness: death.

As I awoke, the earth spiralled up below me. I glided swiftly down, spotting a circle of trees where four wooden benches stood surrounding a soft green mound of earth and grass. The trees, blossoming in pink-white blooms, reflected, shining in the moonlight. I clutched the grass with my claws, stopping high on the side of the mound. Then hopping, half spreading my wings, I jumped to the top of the bench looking out over the inlet. My wings were no longer blue but a mixture of colours of the rainbow; my beak was now a bright orange-red. I was saddened to have to return to this world but my heart sang rejoicing in the freshness and beauty of my spirit.

I looked up through the darkness of night and the stars searching for the golden ring of feathers—when before me, a face began to appear. It was the face of the Medicine Man—dark and gruesome, with eyes like a crow and

## Carrying the Chalice Forward

deep-furrowed wrinkles, covered in paint, speaking of misery and tears. His black hair protruding from under an ancient headdress of an unknown bear: large and ferocious—forgotten since the beginning of time. The hard, wide nose of the Medicine Man was surrounded with powerful lines of red and green paint. His chin was marked with wide stripes of blue—and wide yellow circles filled his cheeks with strength. The Medicine Man's lips and ears were scarred and darkened with age. A fearsome image filled with the pain and suffering of time and with the knowledge and understanding that this pain and suffering bring.

The Medicine Man spoke in an ancient tongue of the spirit world, filling my mind with the meaning and understanding of my many visions—and of my voyage to the island of dreams. I would remain bound to the earth, returning to the spirit world only when I had absolute need or purpose. I would always be able to receive help and assistance from the Great Spirit: the little bird of darkness. I continued to listen as my heart rejoiced in the knowledge that now I was a man: that in the land of my brothers I would be called Great White Eagle—the friend of darkness. The sorrow and gladness of my visions and dreams would be repeated throughout the generations to come.

# Carrying the Chalice Forward

The Medicine Man finished and softly drew away, floating higher, growing smaller and smaller as he returned to the edge of the universe and the island of dreams. I was filled with wonder and excitement at the things I had learned. I knew I could not leave again without first sharing all of my knowledge and new understanding. I looked down and for claws I now had feet; and for wings I now had arms — I was back again.

A grey and white seagull glided through the air and came near. It dropped something dark that landed at my feet. I picked it up: yet it had no substance; it floated in my touch. I brought it closer to put it in my pocket, but as it came near it swept from my hand and plunged into my chest. I could not get it out. It grew and expanded filling me with tremendous power and joy.

I got up and walked along the wooden path beside the inlet, watching the ocean with the sun dancing in sparkles of light amongst the waves. I reflected peacefully on the origin of life and of all things. I stopped: transfixed by the appearance beside me, on my right, of a solid circle of stones laid flat and spread about 20 feet across. In the centre of the floor of stones was a dark mound of earth like a miniature mountain. It stood about two feet high. I wondered at this greatly, for the earth mound was transparent so that I could see the

# Carrying the Chalice Forward

stones beneath it. Out of the side of the mound the forms of animals began to appear and dance around in a circle: a moose, an elk, a deer, a muskrat, a beaver—all dancing to a silent song. Some stood on four legs while others stood upright and many birds and other creatures emerged from the mound to join in the dance. The mound of earth expanded and rose until its base covered the circle of stones.

Inside, the animals continued to dance and grow more numerous every second. The music and beat of the song reached out and filled my heart with happiness. The earth mound continued to rise and spread beyond the edges of the earth, and the universe—leaving behind a transparent veil of darkness that covered everything. I began to sing and rejoice in the song:

> Forget me now while you are here
> and age will pass me by
> Drink a toast and spread some cheer
> and ghosts will never die
> Turn a page and close the book
> and time exists no more
>
> We are free...We are wild
> we dance and shout and sing
> We are the brook...We are the land
> we are what no one holds

Kischi Wapa Keliwa

# Carrying the Chalice Forward

Metis Flag

# 2

# *I am Committed*

# Carrying the Chalice Forward

# 2

One of the potential journeys we are each free to partake of is the teaching of the art of listening to our own souls. To engage ourselves and to begin our own journeys we must each privately take the time to sit quietly and open our hearts and minds to the magnificence of the gifts at the centre of our own souls. We must open our ears to listen to the songs and teachings that rise from the depths of our own silent beginnings and write them down. We may then memorize them so we can pray using our own words or share the songs made for others. By doing so, we learn to walk as an indigenous soul and begin to travel the road to becoming truly free and genuine; despite our separate origins. Our elders have always spoken of the gifts that rise from the depths of our own souls as coming from the heart of creation. Once we reach that quiet space through embracing the maturity of listening, all of creation is reborn anew.

This following song is one my own soul released to me when I asked for my own song. I share it with those who desire to walk their own journeys towards releasing the beauty from within their own souls.

# Carrying the Chalice Forward

## *I am Committed*

I AM COMMITTED
TO THE ONE SPIRIT

IT IS TRUTH

I WALK TOWARDS
THE CENTRE OF MY SOUL

THIS IS MY SONG
PULSING WITHIN ME

I SET IT FREE

I LIVE AND BREATH IT WITHIN ME

I SCREAM IN TERROR
LET IT BE LET IT BE

LET US WALK INTO THE VOID

LET US BE AFRAID

IN TERROR

IN TRUST

IN TRUTH

YAH NAH HAH NAH HEH NAH HAH

YAH NAH HAH NAH HEH NAH HAH

YAH NAH HAH NAH HEH NAH HAH

HEYA

# 3

# *The Song of Culture and Eternity*

# 3

## *The Song of Culture and Eternity*

*I Heard the Eagle call my name.*

*I've listened to the mountain's whisper*

*I've heard the silence of the centuries*

I've heard **Secrets**

In the time when the Great Spirit was naming our brothers, our sisters and the places on the earth, he kept many secrets.

Over time, many of these secrets were taught to the different peoples and animals living in what is now called, the Americas. Some of the secrets, and other things also, were taught to the other peoples and animals of the earth.

As the Great Spirit believed that many of the secrets were too dangerous and powerful for most of the peoples and animals to use at that time, some were kept hidden from everyone.

# Carrying the Chalice Forward

The feeling was that it might be better for the universe if the people of the earth were allowed to destroy themselves first until they had proven that they were ready to learn these secrets to benefit all of life.

The Great Spirit hid many of the secrets deep within the earth. Some of these hiding places have been stumbled upon, as in the old temple and burial mounds, yet, many still remain hidden from both animals and people — underneath centuries of rocks and behind great strong barriers. The Great Spirit was very careful in burying the secrets so that the people and animals would only find them when they had become responsible enough to understand and use the knowledge to benefit all of creation. This is why many of the songs and stories of our great civilizations talk about the underworld and the secrets that are buried there.

What I want to tell you here is a story about two ancient brothers: Culture and Eternity, and how they helped establish the steps that lead us to the secrets of our great civilizations from the past and into the future.

Culture was old before the first people walked the earth. He was born just after his brother, Eternity, who, of course, was born at the start of time. From the very first Culture was in love with life and all things living. His heart would

# Carrying the Chalice Forward

dance and sing at all of the beautiful miracles in great abundance within the creation world. He loved nurturing and helping all forms of life everywhere he went. For many ages Culture travelled the earth and the oceans teaching all of the many living species different ways to survive and prosper.

When Culture met the first people he fell deeply in love with the Daughters of the Earth. He clearly felt that they were very much like him because they taught their children many things to help them survive—and did so for very long periods of time. Culture cherished the Daughters and promised to be near and to help them always.

When Eternity met the first people, he could not understand why anyone would like something that lasted for such a short a period of time. Tortoises lasted 2 to 3 times as long and many trees lived from 5 to 50 times as long. He thought that by the time you were able to learn everyone's name you would have to start over, as most of them would have gone on to the spirit world—so why bother? The main enjoyment for Eternity was to wait for the young children to pass by and jump out at them and scare them. He had lots of fun finding different ways to scare the children, and the rest of the people and animals too. Everyone learned to respect and to fear Eternity and would always run away when they met him.

# Carrying the Chalice Forward

Culture was never really happy with the way his brother treated the children but felt that for some, learning fear might help them to survive a little bit longer. So, for the most part, Culture did not interfere with his brother but let him do his own thing—and stayed as far away from him as possible.

Culture set out to give the Daughters of the Earth abundance in many things. Working day and night he brought the people together into groups so that it would be easier to teach them the skills they each needed to prosper and grow. He taught them all the skills talked of in our old legends and stories. He taught them how to plant, how to make fire, how to sew, how to dance, how to store knowledge, how to communicate—but, most importantly, how to laugh and to be joyful.

After many moons and cycles of ages (as we used to keep track of time), the people had learned many new skills and abilities and proceeded to fill all of the territories provided for them. They had become so great and numerous that Eternity did not even bother to count how many children he scared anymore.

It was at this time that the Great Spirit called an important conference and asked that both Culture and his brother Eternity be present.

# Carrying the Chalice Forward

Eternity was quite glad to go, as he had grown tired of so many, many people and the energy it took to continue to scare all of the young children. Culture, however, was extremely sad and heartbroken, as he had grown very fond of the Daughters and all of their children.

Eternity did not want to bother saying goodbye, so he volunteered to pack the travel gear while Culture went and explained his parting to the Daughters of the Earth. The Daughters agreed to carry on Culture's teaching in his absence and to teach everything they had learned to the children. So Culture and Eternity left the people of the earth with both a happy and a sad heart and began their journey to the conference called by the Great Spirit.

After what seemed a short period of time, the people had become so numerous that they filled all of the territories provided for them and began to wonder what else there was to the earth. The number of people who had gone on to live in the spirit world had become so great a number it was silly to even try to figure it out. The Daughters of the Earth felt they had been having babies forever and had grown tired and bored with the skills they had learned from Culture. In their frustration they turned to the men and bid them to go out and find new skills to keep them happy and free from boredom. The men had to agree and went

## Carrying the Chalice Forward

out in search of new skills for the Daughters of the Earth.

Time went on for many ages of moons and the Daughters were kept quite content with the skills and gifts the men brought continually to their sides. The Daughters became quite lazy about remembering and teaching Culture's teachings and even forgot some of the skills. The men, on the other hand, started to be weary of always being away for such long periods of time. It was then that the men decided to start holding back some of the skills they learned in their travels to try to keep the Daughters happy over longer and longer periods of time. For many cycles of the moon and stars the Daughters were kept quite happy by the new skills they were learning.

Yet, slowly, the Daughters of the Earth began to grow short of temper over small matters and often wondered why they received so few skills when the men now returned and why they did not remain away as long as they used to. They met and held council and all agreed that the men had become extremely lazy. The Daughters agreed that they had best take charge of their own learning and track the men the next time they went out to gather new skills. The council decided to have the men followed the next time they went out.

# Carrying the Chalice Forward

After many attempts to follow the men, one lone child named Troublesome managed to follow them. He tracked them to a secret cave located near two waterfalls. Troublesome watched as the men entered the cave and was able to see them perform many rituals which seemed to allow them to communicate with the spirits in the spirit world. He ran back to the settlement and reported all that he had seen to the Daughters of the Earth.

On hearing this report, all the women grew fearful that perhaps the men had become the beloved of Culture and had stolen the relationship that was meant for them alone. They feared that Culture was no longer happy with them; because they had been lax in their teaching, and even taught skills he had not brought to them. The women feared in their souls that the love meant for them was now forever withheld and was now given only to the men. The women became filled with envy and bitterness towards the men.

The women were now united in a campaign against the men and began to continually mock them for the few skills the men provided and for how inadequate and imperfect these skills actually were. No matter what skill or knowledge the men presented to the women there was always some flaw or imperfection to be found. Soon, the men became worried that perhaps the women were right—that they had

# Carrying the Chalice Forward

become too lazy and did not know anything at all—at least of any worth. The men began to spend more and more time away in their secret cave. Before long the men spent most of their free time away in their cave talking to the spirits.

Through the confusion at having to learn so many imperfect skills the children became bored with learning. They became so annoyed when the teachers tried to teach them another imperfect skill that they would ignore the teachers and play games instead.

The Daughters of the Earth began to doubt their own skills as teachers and turned to the men in anger and frustration. The women blamed their loss of skill on the men and treated them very harshly, indeed. The men responded to this harsh treatment by building many defenses against the women and, of course, spending more and more time hiding in their cave talking to the spirits.

The children were drawn into this ongoing battle and began to fight amoung themselves and to continually harass both the men and the women. Men, women and children all lived in fear of each other and could not hide their anger or their lack of trust for one another. It was at this time that Culture and Eternity returned from their long journey.

# Carrying the Chalice Forward

Both brothers came to visit the peoples living in the territories of the Americas and were amazed at what confronted them. The Daughters of the Earth, on seeing Culture's approach, let out moans and cries and tears flowed down their cheeks. They cried out to Culture to bring again his gifts of prosperity and renewal that would allow everyone to live together again in peace and harmony. Culture, whose heart is as soft as his round clay-like body, was deeply moved and vowed to help the Daughters of the Earth regain their happiness. Eternity, on the other hand, was very disturbed to find that when he popped up in front of the children they didn't run away — some even stuck out their tongues at him and threw rocks.

Eternity sought the council and assistance of his brother, Culture. In council with his brother, Eternity explained his dilemma and asked for Culture's help. Culture only stated that he had never liked the way Eternity would always frighten the young children — and secretly felt that now Eternity was getting the respect he truly deserved. Culture said he would not help his brother.

Not put off by his brother's refusal, Eternity challenged his brother to an all-out wrestling match — the winner to get his own way. Culture secretly felt that his brother must be planning something treacherous, yet could not

## Carrying the Chalice Forward

resist the opportunity of freeing the children from Eternity's nasty visits — it was too much to resist. Culture agreed to the wrestling match on the condition that it take place at the time and place of his choosing. Eternity agreed.

Culture felt that he would have a better chance against his brother's treachery if all the forces of nature were on hand to help in the struggle. So the brothers agreed to meet where the continents of North and South America are joined together.

Eternity, in his all important way, began limbering up for the match and went around flexing his muscles. Because he was so tall he thought by making himself shorter he could increase his power. Every time he made himself shorter the earth would rumble and shake. When he stamped his feet the rocks would fall from the mountain tops and waves appear in the ocean where before there were none. All the people and animals became frightened that perhaps the match was not such a good idea and hoped it would soon be over. Eternity prided himself on his power and strength, thinking that his brother could easily be destroyed now.

Early before dawn Culture rolled his big lumbering body down to the place where the two continents are joined together as one. There he sat peacefully, smoking his peace-

# Carrying the Chalice Forward

pipe, talking with the forces of nature. As dawn approached Eternity lunged out of the darkness and slammed into his brother and together they smashed into the mountains and shook the earth. The dust from their struggle settled on the lakes turning them into mud swamps. Culture would wriggle out of Eternity's grip only to be slammed into once more with the mighty strength of his brother's energy.

Culture looked sideways at the earth and saw the destruction their struggle was causing. He feared that the earth would be destroyed before Eternity tired of his need to win. Culture stretched his outer body to surround Eternity and in this way cushion the earth from the blows and injuries of their struggle.

Eternity was perplexed at Culture's willingness to take the brunt of the blows into his body. Frustrated with the absence or any show of force or struggle, Eternity grabbed hold of Culture's hair and slammed down on his feet and pulled and stretched their bodies up through the clouds, the heavens, the stars — to the edge of the universe; and pushed down on his feet, driving Culture through the crust of the earth, the dark caverns, the underworld — to the centre of the earth. Culture held on with sheer determination and vowed that he would not let the people and animals of the earth

## Carrying the Chalice Forward

suffer through his losing this struggle with Eternity.

Eternity stretched and stretched, pulling his brother's body with him until it was as thin as the silky thread of a spider's web. Culture feared that he would need help now or he would risk snapping in two. He called first on the forces of Earth and Water. Because Culture was so thin and long now, Earth and Water were only able to strengthen him in places. Culture called next on Air and Fire. Fire heated the Air as it blew over Culture's stretched body drying the Earth and Water. Culture then began to bend with the uneven pressure that the spots of Earth caused, bending the body of Eternity in the same way. Like a staircase emerging from out of the darkness, Culture was bending Eternity's straight form with the help of the forces of creation.

Eternity, in his terror, cried out to the Great Spirit for help. The Great Spirit appeared in a great flash of lightning and in a booming voice told Eternity he would now have his wish. The Great Spirit sang a song, giving added strength to the forces of nature and declared that for the rest of time the brothers would remain bound together with the forces of nature so that their source of strength and unity would never be forgotten.

# Carrying the Chalice Forward

Eternity screamed as his body was folded into the emerging shape of Culture's new body.

The Great Spirit boomed a final warning to Culture to beware of the thoughts that being eternal would bring and to hold true to his vow to help the people of the earth to prosper and grow. Like a giant staircase beginning at the centre of the earth and extending to the end of the universe, the bodies of Eternity and Culture were now one.

Culture spoke to the Daughters of the Earth. His voice was very clear, yet not much more than a whisper. He bid the Daughters to have the men and children all become Guardians of the Universe. They must each make a pledge to learn and do what is necessary to maintain and protect the balance of nature in the universe. To accomplish this, the Guardians would have to follow the steps on Culture's body down into the underworld. Once there, they would find the skills and teachings they need to build a united and peaceful civilization.

Culture explained to the Guardians that to enter the universe without destroying ourselves and untold thousands of species and life forms we must unite together as one civilization. We must have mutual respect for one another and for the limits that creation puts on all of existence. We must understand and accept our origins and work together in

## Carrying the Chalice Forward

exploring and inhabiting the universe. We must vow to protect all species and life forms and live in harmony with the forces of creation forever.

If you are ever up before dawn you can still see the evidence of this old struggle between Culture and Eternity. First the dew comes out and covers the standing shrubs and grasses with droplets of water. In each droplet are tiny particles of earth sticking to all of creation. As the sun rises, it heats the air and starts the wind to blow, drying up the droplets of water, hardening the earth. This drying of the morning dew serves as a reminder of the struggle between Culture and Eternity and the forces of creation that bind them together forever. Because this is so you know that this story is true.

*****

This story follows the age-old fight between living and dying, and fear and love.

The forces of nature will fight on our behalf yet we must all follow the steps to ensure our continued connection to the process. Through learning the steps we each must follow we begin to travel the road towards our own divinely-inspired Sovereignty. Understanding that true Sovereignty is living and acting responsibly for everything that happens in the world is a step that has always been expected of our leaders.

# Carrying the Chalice Forward

Following the G20 summit in 2010, the supposed leaders of the world stepped forward to say they were not spending anymore money except on their own salaries and benefits. With the harsh reality of the damage being done, at that time, to the ecosystems and to all the future of life with the oil pouring into the Gulf of Mexico; the true leaders of the world would have pledged the money they had put aside to pay for holding their group-mob meeting and redirected it to pay for fixing at least some of the damage from the oil. True leaders would have done more. When looking at aligning with the true responsibilities of leaders, while embracing a long-term perspective, these leaders are truly an embarrassment. In time one can only hope that common sense will prevail, by our future leaders encompassing and including long-term shared ecological responsibility into economic formulas.

What the current religious and commercial leaders might fail to acknowledge is that at the conference the brothers travelled to, the discussion was about how to remedy the overcrowding of the world and restore balance and harmony with the forces of life. Of great concern were the causes of war and the ongoing suffering of humanity and the impact of humans upon the rest of the creation world. In these discussions the brothers, with

# Carrying the Chalice Forward

everyone and everything else in attendance sculpted the wordings to explain the great laws of tenderness and love (beauty and magnificence); and including also the teachings from the 10 human laws that lead to disharmony, discord and war. These words were written down to help the peoples of the creation world to get along in their now crowded territories. Culture helped sculpt most of the tenderness laws about being in balance with the softer forces of the feminine and gentler nature we each hold, while Eternity relied more on his well-worn teachings of fright and terror to help or hinder humanity in their journey. These primary teachings based on the human causes for war and the matching forces that help bring about prosperity and sacred blessings are those which all of the forces of humanity and nature swore to uphold and share with all of creation forever.

In that ancient time when these were first given to the man on the top of the mountain he was to go forth and to give these to his people. On his way down, after he had put his sandals on and was no longer connected to the sacred earth, he was filled with jealousy and rage at the self-indulgence of his people, so he broke the tablet carrying the laws of tenderness and love. All that his people received were the laws based on fear and compliance. These laws are very limited in their reach and only correspond to the male version of creation and lack much

# Carrying the Chalice Forward

of the tenderness all people and nature crave. Even the Iroquois teach the understanding that men on their own are only capable of destruction. Our combined teachings are that whatever is written from the mind of man alone is incomplete and destructive unless balanced with the female forces that hold a different perspective, and focus on the value of other timeless and gentler aspects of life and creation.

In this we have the choice of which direction or which brother we rely on more for our guidance. Fear establishes order yet does not bring with it beauty and magnificence. When we reach for more than just order we must extend our feeling nature and our connection to the more encouraging forces of creation to again regain the beauty and magnificence at the heart of our loving and sharing communities, present and available to all people the world over.

Many stories of this ancient, white-haired man exist; yet few of them include the telling of who else he was on the mountain with, or who the other participants were as part of the advisory council for the heavens. This man was reportedly a descendant of the families who had followed an old tradition of leaving their homeland. It was ages before, or so it is believed by some, our families had left our homeland of the Americas and travelled and

# Carrying the Chalice Forward

later merged with the Neanderthal-like peoples in an agreement to form a traditional permanent alliance of peace. Our biggest lesson from that journey would seem to be that only through reaching beyond the male perspective for the understanding of our true teachings can we only begin to comprehend the other lessons.

It was said that any who had cause of sufferance, at that time and forever, from any of these issues could come before the leaders of the world and have their voices heard. It has taken many generations of living through conflict, yet the children of this merger still have the greatest challenge to peace in their own attachment to their small-male-minded approach to creation. In seeing the lost nature of his own people while on the mountain, this holy man decided it was best to keep the higher truths for prosperity secret until the people had grown beyond their immature and self-serving nature. Our hope now is that the greater mind in each soul speaks out and inspires the loving demand that peace be upheld and made a permanent bond united with all our families, held through the forces of love and forgiveness forever, the world over.

# Carrying the Chalice Forward

# 4

# *In the Beginning*

# Carrying the Chalice Forward

# 4

In whispering the words of understanding brought to our souls by teachers like Nape, Odin, Zeus, Merlin, the Peacemakers and others we are then free to reflect on the paths we each have to travel in order to re-create our own beginnings. The questions of how we can learn from the indigenous teachings of the Americas and from the teachings of Europeans; and how the dual learning opportunities impact us still today is part of this same wonder of this ancient path some call evolution. The thought of, and even the idea of, "separate races existing" and the secondary thought that "peoples can still exist as independent races" after the known fluid inter-racial movements of our families for thousands of years from all around the world is entirely bizarre. Returning to the truth of our origins and the fully multi-racial history of our more complete story will hopefully humble us all and bring us each the courage to raise ourselves above the gods and heroes of our own making.

Following the old teachings of mixing with other races and nations to strengthen our own families' bloodlines—until there are no boundaries; as we have continually done with those families whose names are long forgotten; and

# Carrying the Chalice Forward

with the Arabs, the Hebrews, the Egyptians, the Greeks, the Turks, the Africans, the Romans, the French, the English, the Portuguese, the Spanish, the Cree, the Algonquin, the Abenaqui, the Huron, the Chippewa, the Assiniboine, the Mandan, the Creek, the Mohicans and others from the north, south, west and east lands. Through this constant intermixing, we have continued to expand the multiracial revolution of whom and what we are as human beings. To embrace the truth of our own origins that stems from the equality within each of our souls, regardless of race or creed, is to bypass all of the propaganda and agendas of those who use racial definitions to control and manage their commercial empires. We are already now so inter-mixed all we need do to embrace the full peace of the world is to remember our true peaceful blood-based alliances formed on terms of full inter-racial equality and embrace our blood-born forgiveness that enables us to heal the rifts of the world and just move forward.

The ideal of erasing the boundaries of race is primarily more of an emotional one than a physical one. The agendas put forward by the commercial empire builders of the crown and religious agencies have confused even our own families. In our needs to survive the destructtion of our economies, peoples and lands, some of our families were forced to take sides and

## Carrying the Chalice Forward

chose amnesia as their way out and forgot our old blood ties for awhile. Things are a bit better now, though with a little less trust and openness. By keeping us scrambling for the morsels thrown at our be-cobbled feet, our would-be captors have forgotten that we have very long memories and stem from an ancient tradition that holds truth and honour as sacred. With little more than the skins on our backs we have merged with great empires through our courage and persistence and have sustained our own part of creation for eternity. The truth of peace and the laws of forgiveness hold us to the path of awareness and our unending duty to love. Our return to expressing love for each other frees us of the bonds of captivity and returns our souls to our rightful inheritance within creation.

Supporting the conscious reality of peaceful co-existence is completely easier once the blood-lines are mixed. It was usually our mothers and grand-mothers who taught us the truth of our existence, although many of our adopted uncles and Moshums taught us our other well-learned truths. Our paternal teachings were more often of the gentle and academic nature played in forming our early identities and loyalties.

The Norman and Celtic French- speaking royal and noble families who chose to enter into permanent blood alliances with the head and

# Carrying the Chalice Forward

chief indigenous families of the Americas comprise most of the main families of the early Bois Brule. Our maternal blood-lines nurtured our indigenous original identity as Bois Brule and helped spread our collective travel and trade alliances from the early east coast families to the far west within just a few generations. The term Bois Brule refers to our maternal Ouendat tradition of burning the brush around our settlements to fertilize our gardens. Our blood ties hold us responsible for upholding the sacred alliances for the land and for the people from one coast to the other and from the north to the south. It is this sacred inheritance running in our veins that calls us to care for all of the land and for all of the people of our combined inheritance. In good Conscience, our old and true families continue to listen to their hearts and still hold all of the lands and peoples of all our ancestors and cousins as sacred and holy.

Peaceful co-existence does not actually mean subjugation and extermination; it really means share and share alike. Disease and weaknesses are overcome, as the Royal Society took note of as early as 1810, through the mixing of territorial-based indigenous bloodlines with the bloodlines of the visiting newcomers. These cross-breeds or half-breeds, as we often refer to ourselves as, retain the newcomer's resilience to the diseases they bring with them and the

# Carrying the Chalice Forward

strength and durability of the indigenous ways. Through the acceptance and nurturing of cross-breed alliances our non-indigenous and indigenous cousins benefited tremendously from the alliances formed through the unions of our parents. In full accord with long-standing traditions, the chief and head families were often required to offer their offspring for mutually beneficial alliances. In this way our families were and are still of great and mutual benefits to our ancestors' original families, as long as we are of the mind of sharing.

Our old families' references to marriage agreements often held them to be treaties, as between sovereigns, and regarded us as the emissaries of peace for travel and trade between our different families' territories. Because we travelled and traded over such a wide and diverse territory (From the bottom of Florida to Great Bear Lake in the north and from Newfoundland to Vancouver Island) our families and alliances very quickly included the majority of all the indigenous families from one ocean to the other. Our kokums taught us the traditions of sharing and cohabiting within the lands of our cousins and how to be true offspring of the Creator. Each of these alliances created offspring that travelled with our families to our summering supply posts and back again to our traditional wintering grounds. The old settlements of Cincinnati, Kansas, Pennsylvania, Kentucky, Oregon,

# Carrying the Chalice Forward

Miami, Green Bay, Red River, Pembina, Athabasca and others each bear testament to our historic ties and activities there. Our multi-territorial inheritance bound with our indigenous traditions and multi-linguistic inheritance created and merged all of our families with the original indigenous spirit of the land. We have never stopped being the emissaries of peace and still hold to the responsibility for the reciprocal alliances of the families within all of our shared territories across both Canada and the US.

It was the pledges of familial allegiance that provided the true, traditional and lasting forms of peaceful union. It was and is not just that we are the descendants; we are the inheritors of the indigenous lineages of our mothers and grandmothers, fathers and grandfathers. When we travel to or live in our traditional family regions of the Algonquin, Huron, Iroquoian, Big Belly, Lakota, Chippewa, Cree, Creek, Blackfoot and other territories, that our families had previously agreed to live in and share together as one, we are doing so under our own true indigenous rights of inheritance. We are their descendants and hold our full indigenous responsibilities, titles and rights from these women and men. As we are primarily a travelling and trading family, our travelling homes are the rivers and campsites from one side of Turtle Island to the other.

## Carrying the Chalice Forward

The indigenous concept of merging as allies includes the individual ability to be dual citizens. The French understood this quite well and allowed and supported our families' holding of full citizenry, with the right to own land and obtain licenses; and equally our rights to be full-blooded indigenous people as dually registered citizens. Chief Pachirini is one such example where as headman of the Petite Nation of Algonquin he received full French title, in the form of a fiefdom, to his family's indigenous homeland on and around Alumette Island. The indigenous families, amoung whom lived the Norman French speaking trading families of Normandy and France, gave these Normans the same right to the use of the land and the entitlement to food and to be heard as the rest of the indigenous families.

The French had a tradition of god-parenting allies, as in the case of LaVerendrye's full-blooded Algonquin great uncles, Joseph and Jean Baptiste Saguirou, who became Gauthiers and were licensed as French fur traders to the west as early as 1690. As licensed French citizens they were allowed to own property and to gain protection from the French Militia if required. Their descendants continued to intermarry with the Algonquin, Cree, Chippewa and others, helping to form an intricate web of connections throughout the northern families and helped with some of the push for the emergence of the Bois Brule

# Carrying the Chalice Forward

families. There are many instances of our family groups being admitted or adopted into the French from many of the eastern, southern, northern, plains and western tribes. The indigenous tradition of increasing the strength of the family through using the resources at hand (whether they looked different or not) was good; as long as they were capable of, at least, pretending to be human. If they said they wanted to be part of our family, the tradition was to extend them the trust in the belief that the Creator must have had a purpose for every part of existence: and you could not fault creation for inspiring them to come forward to help bring new bloodlines into the families. The adopted families were never lost to the alliance as they enshrined the bloodlines with our allies and their descendants were a gift of the Creator to enhance and uphold the peace and provide permanent benefit for all the families involved. The children, born of these unions, more often than not, became the main family chiefs and headmen and headwomen within the next and following generations.

The true concept of share and share alike was alive and well with the Norman, French, Scottish and other Celtic settlers and traders. Their inherent love of wine, women and song did them a great service and encouraged the ease of their intermarriages, so much so, that most early Canadians who have done proper

## Carrying the Chalice Forward

genealogies will find their own indigenous roots and connections in more cupboards than the tailor has shoes. The concepts of the English, with their hard-line bureaucratic approach towards racial mixing, were entirely different. Their race-based domination theory tendencies; and their lack of expertise in the arts of wine, women and song; would keep them in the dark ages until the time of the Beatles and the emergence of the age of free love, and the subsequent softening of these outmoded boundaries. Now that the English are coming of age into the light of peace and love through sharing, we can begin to welcome them to surrender to the equality of love and begin walking this road to enter the true new world as part of our family.

Our own families' journey out of secrecy to merge our cause with the old indigenous sacred foundations of Hochelega, by building the new Mont Royal (Montreal); was a testament to our true families' encompassing of a humane vision for a united, peaceful world. As the English and their allies held a different vision of humanity, and wanted to be the bosses of the world, they chose to be the enemies of the true peace. The ongoing commitment to work with the Algonquins, Hurons and other indigenous families as Allies; and to embrace the real humanity of the indigenous soul as worthy of love and protection - and vice a versa, was at the heart

## Carrying the Chalice Forward

of the semi-spiritual movement inspiring the spirit and heart of the land and of the people who chose Mount Royal as their Sacred Haven. As in the times and through the same bloodlines of Noah, a new humanity was created through the merger of our indigenous families' blood-lines from both the old and new worlds. The Bois Brule are just one part of the worldwide exeunt genesis of our family.

The master builders in the guise of D'Alleboust, along with the Gauthiers, Marins, Bouchers and others of the time; committed to building the hospitals, and helped provide the infra-structures of defense needed in order to live peaceably in the shared territories. The ongoing involvements of the other families including the Cooks, Caris, Caens, Chabots, Denys, Baudouins, Biencourts, Godfreys, Martins and others, provided the economic push to allow the humane co-development to continue until the indigenous and noble families merged and encompassed each other's bloodlines. In this a new humanity was born--a concept that the English and other near-sighted nationalistic families missed the point of. The true vision of the new humanity was to help lay the foundation for the co-creation of a humanely conscious community built on caring, peace, love and sacred respect for life. This true peace was later to envelop nearly 100 indigenous family nations culminating in the Great Peace of 1701.

# Carrying the Chalice Forward

The early French-speaking and indigenous families did not exclude someone from being human, from the highest to lowest, if their skin was able to hold a tan longer. Most indigenous traditions, especially in Huronia, encouraged the joining of new families. It was more in reaction to success of the mixed blood families that the church and state adopted and instituted their racial approaches to exclusion from land ownership for "tainted" individuals, so that certain or other, somewhat "untainted" families could take control of the land. The early examples of this are what happened to our cousin Sieur Denys in Acadia. It was primarily with the English and the churches who equated being of indigenous blood as a sin and punishable by legislation. The 1885 Department of Education Canadian history handbook specifically refers to "the tainted blood of Louis Riel" as from "that savage race" in describing to good Canadian citizens: exactly what was a respectable genealogy. Many of our cousins who, before this rise in prejudice, would acknowledge their mixed-blood heritage and connections to our families, became afraid for their own commercial and social survival; and worked hard to hide any connection to their "tainted" mixed-blood past. The churches quite equivocally made it a sin as much as if one had had Hebrew parents, and urged mixed-blood parishioners to hide and distance themselves from their past con-

## Carrying the Chalice Forward

nections and become white farmers and industrialists instead of Metis or Bois Brule. Yet still, our blood speaks out from our very cells and compels us to stand for our true full bloodline inheritance and bring forward our gifts for the benefit and healing of the entire world.

The original merger of our bloodlines, with the caring and sharing of our own real humanity, still stands forth as our family's unending gift to the indigenous world. Although we have endured the effects of racism, legislated expulsions and theft of our homes and economies; as well as the viscous effects of segregation and virtual captivity, we have still survived. The Jesuits, and other cloak wearers, did not know what to do with us: as they had less power in the new world than they had at Bisors or Mont Segur; yet they did, however, still hold the power of the inquisition; and had many of our families swear abjurations in order to be able to enter into the territory. Facing these disadvantages for a time has strengthened our resolve, as it did Abraham, and has ushered us on into this new age so that now in this eco-friendly, socially-conscious atmosphere of encouragement and hope for humanity and the world, we are stepping forward to remove the mountains of racism and greed from all of humanity's path.

## Carrying the Chalice Forward

It was not until the emerging English bureaucracy realized that our families already inhabited the main thoroughfares of the country, and that only through the coveting of these properties, that were owned or controlled by the wealthy mixed-blood merchant families, that the real race-based struggles began. By legislating our identity, and rights of legal existence, into obscurity: where mixed bloods could not inherit legal title under English law; and could not become a vassal of the crown unless they surrendered their independence and rights of inheritance (which were only obtainable after many years of court battles), we entered a stage of virtual captivity under English law.

The original mergers, however: based on true love and acceptance, are the fulfillment of the visions of our traditional indigenous elders and head families; and are the real foundation of the spirit and heart of the new world. Emerging from the heart of creation to help protect the earth and its inhabitants from the continuing warfare and greed of the spoiled children, who currently call themselves leaders, is the fulfillment and entrenchment of our birthright. Besides leading the line-ups to get their paycheques at the banks, these current leaders also seem to be first in the line-ups to place blame on everyone else for the continued destruction of the natural world - as is still happening in the Gulf of Mexico. True

# Carrying the Chalice Forward

leaders understand that they hold, entirely and fully, the responsibility to look after all aspects of the world—not just their own private agendas. It is only through embracing the Great-minded approach of our indigenous families: of all sitting and working at the same table for the safeguard and protection of our worldwide human community, in sacred balance with all life, and on equal terms with each other; that the full vision of peace will be realized.

With time, and a little push by the Creator, the true terms of peace, acceptance and forgiveness will spread as a blossom from our hearts to embrace the entire world with the beauty of love and tenderness. This is our inheritance and our truth; as heard echoing through the dreams of Abraham, Ishmael, Isaac, Lot, Buffalo Calf-robe Woman, Mary, Odin and other Patriarchs and Matriarchs of our families: to hold true to our love of one another and face our innocence and our guilt together in freedom for the Greater purpose of all humanity.

As the descendants of the embodiment of our family's worldwide conscious endeavour to merge with the indigenous families; as our families had previously merged with the Norwegian, Goth, English, Roman, Moslem, Greek, Turkish and other families throughout history; the expression of the true teachings of

# Carrying the Chalice Forward

peace and prosperity, through union and acceptance and full undeniable equality as fellow human beings, is enriched and fulfilled. Through the indigenous women, and the families accepting the alliances of full unions by marriage, their children extend the continual blessings of their united ancestors through infusing the history of the world and the foundations of human conscience with the true inheritance of all the ancestors. As descendants of the inherent, traditional and sacred heads of families of the old world; and the traditional indigenous heads of families in the new; the responsibilities to hold both worlds and all peoples as sacred is in our blood and in our bones. Holding forth our visions in alignment with the visions of our patriarchs and matriarchs, as we carry forward the stone of our freedom, will ignite the will of the people to stand tall and free; and is the fulfillment of our reaching beyond our smallness to embrace the ancient dream.

In our indigenous hearts we may ask, "What on earth were our ancestors thinking? When they agreed to the alliances with the visiting families from across the waters?" We must then search and reach for the understanding of their vision, and hopefully their path, for us. We may also ask the same of the Creator. The answers will undoubtedly reflect the real indigenous views we are each striving to comprehend.

When we go back to the early writings of

# Carrying the Chalice Forward

Champlain's time we find that our family's stated hope for us was through the peaceful joining of our families into a united offspring that shared the land and the resources as one family. The strength of our translation of these early visions can really only be measured in how united we have become as a family; and in how much honour we have, and do, contribute towards their vision for us. What can be discerned from the racial interference of the English and Papal agendas is that they, especially, did not want any descendants to claim anything permanent to do with dual inheritance. As a result, the dilemma our families faced, and are still facing, was that to be pro-peace we must support the unions of our families; to be pro racist we must support the agendas of the church and the English bureaucracy. In this issue there was, and is, left no middle road; as the original vision was very clear: in that peace is held as the inherent right of the descendants, and the original branches of our families are obligated to support that peace.

The visions and the reality of pursuing the goal of co-creating a new humanity from the union of the families can only be fully entertained when held in our higher consciousness. The ongoing and current challenge has been, that with the needs to survive keeping us more often in our small mind, we have sometimes hindered our own family's progress toward

## Carrying the Chalice Forward

fulfilling the original vision. Yet, when we step back and view the overall worldwide close-knit familial alliances spreading out from the sacred hills and mounds of our heritage; the long-term reality is that, at our heart, our families from the four corners of the world care for the health and balance of the forces of life on the earth and are listening to this internal indigenous voice in our souls bringing us all back to the same table.

How clear our hearts are and how much we are of the same Great Mind will determine how long it takes for us to act to help the earth regain the balance needed to sustain life for future generations.

Our true indigenous obligation is to honour the women of our inheritance and learn what we can of their original families and traditions, and re-teach these to our children and our families. Whether they were known just as Susan, Marie, Angelique, or even just Amerindian; they are our sacred blood bearers and dream teachers. The loyalty and nobility in the blood of our indigenous forebears guides and moves us ever onward. Listening to the dreams and teachings that these maidens bring to our waking mind awakens the true power of our vision and empowers each of us with the strength of the angels to move through and surmount all of our challenges. The oldest and hardest teaching for men to hear is that the women always win and always know what it is we truly want.

## *In the beginning*

In the beginning
was the wyrd
and the wyrd was with Odin
and it was good

now others claim origin of the wyrd
who do not descend from the way
but from their own folly
and they are not good

Without connection to fathir and mothir
or grandfathir or grandmothir
the way is easily lost
and the path to follow very confused

were it not for the strength of fenrir
little children would lay full claim to the throne
and jormungand would perish in the flames
and yggdrasil turn to ashes

yeh this maiden who hearkens us each time
filling our hearts with the courage to resist
the game of paradise destruction
played by the children who have no soles

# Carrying the Chalice Forward

Yet walk on their toes through the burning ashes
tearing great holes in sacred palaces
where are they gone? — these child like anguishes
there are no remnants in the souls of our toes

We walk yet awhile heretofore the way
to trust in our hearts forgiveness through the day
of balancing the beam astride our grey horses
that cares for the world with all the life forces

In harmony we say is gently found the way
to return to our mothir and play with our fathir
on our journey ever home to grandfathir and grandmothir
through the fields of our dreams and visions of our souls

In the end all actions must be atoned for and balanced with love. Through forgiveness, as our teachings hold; and as the great law also shows, we must console all of the individuals and families to bring their hearts and minds back to that state of peace that we have always relied on for true forgiveness and acceptance. It is this sacred, peace-supporting and indigenous-based community we each crave. There is only true community when such equalities are supported; and the repairing and balancing forces of life are allowed to rebuild

# Carrying the Chalice Forward

the beauty of creation, with strength enough to sustain all of our lives in growth and abundance. We are responsible for more than just standing by and watching, we must act and hold our souls in our inheritance of the great-minded vision and step forward to help the earth with our lives and our love. We can only do so together in total forgiveness and peace with the shared knowledge and acceptance of beauty and joy as our only rightful inheritance.

# Carrying the Chalice Forward

# 5

# *In the Houses of the Holy Blood*

# Carrying the Chalice Forward

# 5

This song was written in honour of our family's visions together as we awaken to this new version of the dream from inside our own journeys through the darkness, and from inside our own internal struggles to be and remain free. We enjoin many mysteries in this journey we call life: some make us laugh, others cry; yet many fill our souls with awe. Laughter is, for me, the most telling: as the same tricks have been played on us all. Only the Creator knows for sure how much laughter we can each handle at any one time.

## *In the Houses of the Holy Blood*

In the houses of the holy blood
you have mysteries and secrets galore
Free from the vicissitudes of time
A shrine to our heaven is built
Wherein lies our mother the sun
Hearkened on her journey through dark
Astride her stead white shining alabaster
Into the tunnel she goes
Where doth wander her lieges and enemies
more
In darkness crying pain and bitter woe

# Carrying the Chalice Forward

Astride her stead she comes again
Whither doth she wander and count her foe
Astride the moon she counters woe
For in the veil her children grow
A count our numbers you will know
For here and far we rise again
A peaceful horde of free women and men

# Carrying the Chalice Forward

# 6

# *Four Astride a Horse*

# Carrying the Chalice Forward

# 6

In the achieving of who or what we are in this great big universe; and how we each come to our own point of exercising the full creative power living within us, is in our individually coming to the starting point of our own unique and true journey. Coming to know what is real is part of this great journey into understanding; what it is we have been taught, what it is we have experienced, what it is we have hoped for; and, especially, what it is we have begun. By releasing our collective soul's vision from within each of us, we begin the journey into understanding what it is to be truly indigenous.

In one of my own visions, after searching through some writings describing the archetypes of the creative force within each of us, I clearly discerned an image of four people on the back of a horse. The translation and words of that vision are here shared for your pleasure. Through repetition of these words in song or prayer, as the elders have often tried to teach us, the power of the forces of creation are called upon to help transform the world. With the power inherent in our heart-based expressions we are each capable of calling on the forces of creation to expand and transform our own souls to begin flowing in unison together;

## Carrying the Chalice Forward

thereby expanding the beauty inherent in the expression of our own boundless will.

The belief is that through understanding the archetypes, which make up the human soul; and through using the forces which give us the inspiration to direct our own expressions, we become free to exercise our combined creative force to fully express ourselves in alignment with our own unique soul's journey. Whether these are the archetypes designed to help us understand and learn to travel the path to true freedom or just teachings towards learning a higher definition of ourselves, the validity of what they embody is easily relevant.

One of the greatest contributions toward the conscious awakening of the collective indigenous soul within each of us is the strengthening of the dream to continue the creation of a better world. All souls working in unison to create new ways to move forward in peace, draw on the forces of creation and the miracle of our own understanding of the true vision of the new world. Accomplishing the ending of hate or anger at the past will undoubtedly help the world to move forward into the real expression of peace: with all beings together flying the same flag of love. As hokey as it sounds, the only song we can sing as evolved human beings, is one of co-creation through the force of love.

# Carrying the Chalice Forward

We are the people of the horse: the eternal buffalo people, the free people; Otipemisiwak; the children of the patriarchs of peace. We are like the star children spoken of in many songs and stories. Many of us stand out and unsettle our sometimes confused cousins by how versatile we can be and how we sometimes seem to speak a different language of understanding.

While speaking at a Metis symposium in Ottawa many years ago, a cousin shared a portion of a manuscript she had located from a museum that talked about our Bois Brule/Metis women riding horses, and about a man who was supposedly Louis Riel in hiding in 1870 in Montana.

The women (5 or 6 of them) were out riding on the western plains and stopped in to one of the local saloons to quench their thirst. They roped off their horses and strode into the saloon. The men, on seeing the Metis women: moved away from the bar, left their seats, moved to the back tables and left the women in peace. Each of the women strode up and dropped their Winchester rifles onto the bar and were duly handed their whiskeys. They finished up their drinks, shook the dust off their shoulders, paid their money and went on their way. Riding off on their horses the way you are supposed to ride—with a leg on either side. The men crawled back to their seats and resumed their

# Carrying the Chalice Forward

day. Within 20 years our men were forcing these same women, through the pressures of the church and the state, to wear petticoats and to stay home.

Another tale was that in the descriptions of Riel, renamed as Robidoux for the story, while in hiding in Montana, he had with him a young consort. When I asked my cousin if the young woman's name was Josephte and about 20 years old, she said, "Yes she was." When I laughed and said, "That was my great, great grandmother," we laughed some more. The description was of a scantily clad Riel and Josephte jumping off of each others shoulders in a waterfall-fed pool having a grand old time.

The description made perfect sense, as our Great, great, great grandfather: Solomon Hamelin, who was the main head of the French-speaking Metis in Red River at the time, was the one who was known for protecting Riel and showing him the buffalo hunt; which Riel had never experienced as a youth. Solomon and his sons and daughter were proud of what Louis had done to help the families and the budding arrangement seemed pleasing for all.

Something did happen, though, and the connection ended. Josephte married a different Metis man and the Hamelin's broke ties with Riel. Solomon's son even ran against Louis in

# Carrying the Chalice Forward

the seat for parliament and won, serving for 11 years, representing the Metis families, as the MP for the J.A. MacDonald Conservatives. The understanding was that our families had asked Riel not to grandstand anymore and to just do things peacefully.

When Mussolini gained power temporarily in Italy, the Metis families sent him a white stallion on which to ride into battle, as the hoped for triumphant soldier of the apocalypse. We did not know he would become a tyrant. In the same way we did not know Napolean would become lost in his own imaginings. Finding leaders who trust and speak of ideals rooted in our hearts and hopes all face the same dilemma of also being small-minded humans who easily get lost in the dark.

Through reaching beyond the limited perception of the world based on our own small-minded beginnings, we can gain the foothold into the heart of creation, thereby allowing what is in our visions to come forward through the night into our consciousness. From our conscious beginnings, beyond just grabbing control of the land and the people, we can embrace our good conscience and debate the terms of forgiveness and prosperity; which lay the foundations for the enrichment of the new world on the terms of love and based on the principles of peace.

# Carrying the Chalice Forward

The pope and the church wardens seemed to have often mistaken possession of the land, and of the people, for peace; when in truth: the freedom of the people and the sacred holding of the land are everyone's perpetual inheritance of greater purpose; and the only true path to follow. Because the souls of the other lands forgot their indigenous blood bond to the land and people, does not mean that they are not bound by indigenous responsibilities; or that they are somehow forgotten. All it means is that the balance of life ever tips away from the cold-hearted and the greedy, to await the desire of the true people to return the sacred balance of the world: as it was written and agreed to at one point by all indigenous people; and is still held in sacred trust, for all of life, within the heart of creation.

For our families, the symbol of the horse lives on as very ancient and powerful medicine. The growing knowledge of the healing powers of this co-operative, herbivore, and the greater knowledge of its long tried approach to survival and existence, is bound to the heart of the indigenous dreams for the future. The following song speaks of the power within each of us, and our horses - or "our vehicles of power", from which we may each draw upon to gather the strength needed to follow our soul's true path towards balancing our inner dreams and belief systems. This balance is attained through accessing the full powers of creation from within the depths of our own individual souls. Our learning and teaching is that we each give honour and strength to our journey's purpose through our conscious return to the sanctity and sacredness of our own souls.

We are each capable of praying, as our elders and ancestors have taught us: from the words that rise from the heart of our own souls. Some prayers and songs we are free to share so that others may learn of our soul's teachings, and of the paths we may walk together, bound with the grace and beauty of creation. We freely share this song for those who desire to gain purpose and gentleness in the fulfilling of their own journeys.

## FOUR ASTRIDE A HORSE

Four Astride A Horse
In Single File
Who I am I ask

**One Who Knows All**
**A Maiden — All In White**
The Centre of My Soul

**A Wise and Strong Brave**
**One Who Wears a Crown**
A Vision Most Renown

# Carrying the Chalice Forward

Ask Yourself Who I Am
In a Dream You'll See
The Meaning of **Who is Me**

Reframe Your Life
Frame Your Escape
To the Renewed Hope

Of a Dream Far Away
Past the End of Your Nose
Only a Step Away

**Take the Plunge**
**Run and Lunge**
**Tear the Fabric of your Soul**

**Be Strong and Brave**
**Envision a New You**
Forever Strong and True

In a Dream without End
Always More to Be
The Keepers of Your Soul

Keep the Dream Going
Like a River Ever Flowing
From Who I Am to Me

Keep the Faith
Act Now — Don't Wait
**Your Hero's a Strong Desire**

# Carrying the Chalice Forward

To Contemplate
The Reason Why
**We All Must Fly**

And Bring About
This Very Hour
Of Dreams Come True

For in this Vein
We Strike Again
The Candle of Renew

Upon the Light
That Guides our Soul
From Holy Me to Holy New

Amidst this Dream
To Create Again
Our Soul's Desire

Astride our Horse
We Ride Again
Through Burning Fire

# 7

## *Pharaoh's Dream*

# Carrying the Chalice Forward

# 7

## PHARAOH'S DREAM
And the dawning of the age of good conscience
REMEMBERING THE TRUTH OF OUR NOBILITY

Since the time of the Red-Headed Pharaohs, and before, the dreams of Mighty Pharaoh have held hope for our believing in the creation of a peaceful and prosperous world. When the crescent moon flies low over the southern shores we are drawn to recount the telling of these dreams, to remember the origins of peace; and of the true passages of power.

In olden times, as some may remember, the South was known as the top of the world and all things revolved around events in that hemisphere. The South has always been kept sacred to our families and other peoples. The old saying of: "not knowing which way is up," can be said to possibly mirror this old understanding. The big question though, in this over-engaged and irresponsible era, is whether truth is still truth? Following the telling of so many distorted and misleading understandings—created by the darker forces of the world of self-serving agendas, how can we discern what we have been told to be true?

# Carrying the Chalice Forward

In that old time, when Pharaoh looked down to the northern shores many people held a different view of the world and had not yet become so co-dependant. These stories recount how the original people gained, in truthful reality, their soul-based independence and freedom—and are still this way today. The scary part of remembering these stories, and the truth of what we have been told, through listening with our hearts to what we know is true, is like peeling away many layers of lies and deceptions to reveal our own complicity in creating the world as we find it today. Our understanding is that it is in becoming responsible for our own divinity, and for how our thoughts and actions affect the world, that we come face to face with our own folly; and can then accept the repercussions of our own self-serving journeys through the tortuous valleys of dependence and need.

The remedy that some can choose to follow is to stay as children: so they can still receive the returns of the commercial world, and leave their conscience asleep—that is their free choice. Our hope is that through embracing the laws of tenderness, and binding our souls to the preserving actions of the protection and renewal of all life on earth, we awaken the dream of our divinity and become as pharaoh. Our understanding is that in the depths of our souls we each hold the choice of whether to

# Carrying the Chalice Forward

embrace each other with total love, and to willingly act in support and encouragement of love for all life for all time, or to stay as the unwrapped onions we were born to be.

In these old times, Pharaoh had dreams. The dreams shocked Pharaoh and changed him. His mind and heart were troubled and out of step with his own people. In the dreams he had visions of one land rising up and merging into and combining with another. In these lands he walked amoung his people and, as he looked, *with eyes veiled in the dream world*, he gasped at the vision: as each face turned into an image of Pharaoh; mirroring him in all his various activities and functions. He trembled as he noticed they each wore the royal garments and each held his staff of power in their hands.

Everywhere he looked he saw multitudes of images of himself and as they looked through him with their cat-like eyes, he withdrew into his own imagination and grew silent. He seldom left the safety of his caverns to journey amoungst the people. He became as a child. He reviewed the images of his dream and wondered at his own true connection to the world and to all people.

The dreams came to him each night through several seasons. He talked to his counsellors and advisors; who offered little or no comfort. He journeyed to, and walked through, the

# Carrying the Chalice Forward

caverns beneath his temple searching for answers. He beheld many wonders in his visions. Everywhere he looked he saw reflections of himself. Each vision and spirit was unique and self-contained. As no one could dare to look him in the eye, at least without being executed for such insolence; he began to question the very laws that kept order and balance around him. He began even to question the source of his own authority.

He wondered about his own people and how they would act if they were each pharaoh? How could these people, who were not much more capable than simple rats and dogs, ever hope to do what he could do? How could they take soul journeys to the land of the dead? Or talk to creatures from the other worlds? Or heal the sick with a touch, or a thought? — Or ever kill with just the look of an eye? Or wield the true power as only Pharaoh can?

At that time, it was only the enlightened, or those who had crossed the bridges between the worlds and waded in the streams of infinity or grasped the reigns from the hands of Time herself, who could truly become like Pharaoh. Only a select few could be called human/divine enough to be capable of even communing with Pharaoh. The world did not make sense otherwise. If everyone was Pharaoh what lie of the universe could bring this about? Or what truth would extend such power to the

## Carrying the Chalice Forward

people? How could what was always and forever taught no longer be true?

His food, and even his divine work, became chores and he lost the joy he had once received from even simple things.

In part of the vision there were four pillars that he had walked between; yeh, a fifth—that matched the four in width. On each were written symbols that he alone could read. These were like the sacred symbols written in the script of the burial glyphs from the ancient crypts. Each symbol represented one of the principles of heaven and the fabric that bound them all together and acted on them. As he watched; all the people walked through the pillars, and entered into them. After merging through the pillars, each person adorned himself or herself with the garb of Pharaoh and greeted him with the noble sign.

On the final day, after the cycle of the seasons, a child appeared to Pharaoh to welcome him on to a well-marked road that meandered through the empire. Following this road, Pharaoh moved across distant lands to villages with homes made of wood and straw, quite a very long distance away. There, Pharaoh sat with the princes of the families and broke bread with them in celebration and in honour of his visit. Pharaoh sat and communed with these princes who welcomed him and bid him

# Carrying the Chalice Forward

to be happy. He felt great peace. Pharaoh removed his crown and left it at their feet. At that time, the child turned to Pharaoh and said, "Now it is complete - you may go."

Pharaoh regained his vigour and his joy, yet never again looked at his people with the same disregard. He did not trust in their possible divinity, yet he no longer denied it.

Through time, as all of the children spread forth from Pharaoh, the earth and heavens become more and more under the impact and influence of the emergence of the divine human. Just as other generations had previously spread forth from leading icons like Odin or Zeus, bringing forward new understandings of the divine human emergence, the divine world known to each age has kept changing. Our eternal questions have pretty much remained the same: What does it truly mean to be noble and divine? To whom do we answer? What are our true roles in creation? Are we free or tamed — or in prison? What happens when we change?--Are we still the guiding forces for humanity? If so, what are we going to do to help the world and give strength to the forces of life to triumph over the destructive forces we have helped create during our childish times?

The small mind (the ego) belonging to every human is known as the sole source of the

## Carrying the Chalice Forward

destructive energy of the world. In the ego exists the ignorance and selfish focus that excludes the compassion we need as the higher beings we are, or are capable of being, to protect the balance of the living forces. We alone are responsible for the rest of life because we know the impact we have and are having upon the world. The Iroquois refer to these forces as the unbridled male forces without the guiding and tendering influences of the women. Pharaoh's dream holds one portion of the key to expanding our understanding of our current world's journey, and how we can apply our divine human forces to fulfill our sacred responsibilities.

Pharaoh returned from his journey complete in his understanding that even those who live in simple ways are capable and able enough to become noble and divine. The pillars of passage, he felt, are fully open for all people to pass through to learn the secrets of living and dying; and how to rise above and beyond all of our limitations to become as Pharaoh. The Creator, from eternity, has provided these paths for all beings who desire to enter into the mysteries of life and begin their own journeys to become human/divine expressions of living. Yet, in this, Pharaoh knew he understood very little of the people. He knew that in his desire to fulfill the purpose of his dream he would need to surrender his crown and authority for a short season—or, at

# Carrying the Chalice Forward

least, until his own journey was nearly complete.

One understanding of hope for the new world is that Pharaoh's, Abraham's, Quetzalcoatl's, and the Peacemaker's blood lines have become fully joined. In this way the seed of Adam, and Nape, (Oldman), are joined forever. Today the Metis, Metzitos, Aboriginal and Inuit families hold the rest of the keys for achieving and maintaining world peace and prosperity. Through the old alliances and dynastic marriages arranged with the majority of the indigenous families our combined families now can be seen to represent the free peoples of the world.

One of the hurdles to peace is that in the brokering of the merger of our territories, the English chose to oppose our families and subjugated our economies and peoples as captives to their commercial empire. The next 250 years witnessed the culmination of the playing out of the greed and racism based on the Roman ideal of totalitarian conquest. In this way, the established order of cultural merging based on alliance and peace was overturned. Instituting the English versions of feudal law for the territories over shadowed the existing peace and laid the ground rules for the current forms of governance and claims to title to the Americas. Now, for our families to return to the same table, in this time of interdependence,

## Carrying the Chalice Forward

we will need to be set free and provided an equal spot at the table. Whether the so called leaders of the world are ready for this, or not, still remains to be seen.

Now that all of our collective families are waking up to their indigenous obligations and responsibilities to the majority of the peoples and territories of the world, the roots of peace are gaining new strength. It is only through this true honourable peace and the faithful meetings and honouring of souls at the same table as equals, in full surrender of all false or real claims to title; that the age of peace will fully be able to be born.

It is our further understanding that anything short of a full surrender to the great laws of peace, with good minds and hearts, will end with the almost total decimation of life on the earth. The teachings are that the great law is written into the fabric of the universe as the permanent and perpetual guide for this age, for all people. A portion of these laws were used to help form the original foundation of the United Nations. Yet, still, what is missing is the full inclusion of the true noble and sacred families: whose responsibility it is to help guide this age forward. Such is our teaching and our desire for peace that we hold still the eagle feather, forever tied to the staff of power, binding us together walking softly on this earth as a family united in the same dream.

# 8

*Letting Go
of Paradise*

# Carrying the Chalice Forward

# 8

For centuries, one of the old challenges to peace has been the gap between the indigenous life-honouring traditions and the religious world's dogmatic views: of the beginning of life, the workings of creation and what happens to us when we die. The pope and other agencies were very thorough to voraciously attack the indigenous idea of the Creator and forcefully impose the concept of a vengeful god. Their ongoing efforts to eliminate the happy hunting grounds and other afterlife beliefs and practices dogged our traditional teachers for ages. The religious agencies even enlisted the help of their commercial partners to take over the pseudo-ownership and control of our physical bodies through various legislations, along with other similar legislations aimed at halting the native ceremonies and traditions surrounding the afterlife. Today, the growing consciousness and compassionate awareness for other people's beliefs and customs has re-opened a great door for us to freely overcome these old challenges and begin the long path towards healing.

The work toward overcoming these legislations and race-based agendas is being carried on through all the different levels of our

# Carrying the Chalice Forward

family; and eventually will help smooth the steps in this cooperative journey towards forgiveness and peace.

This following mantra/song rose up from my soul in answer to my own prayerful questions of: Why, if the Creator truly loves us, were so many people allowed to die in the last 500 years? — as part of the papal-sponsored aggressions into the new world? (Our indigenous population in the 1500s was greater than that of China). The deaths occurred primarily through the introduction and advent of the old-style diseases, brought to the indigenous families, both purposefully and accidentally. Basically $1/5^{th}$ of the world's population died in less than 100 years. Our world was not perfect, yet some things were a lot better than much of what we have experienced since. If the lesson for us to learn is that the Creator has always loved us, and still loves us, and all we need to do is sit still and listen to the answers to the questions from our hearts, then so be it. The answer I received to my own prayers was to transform our own lives, and express the light in our souls to the world; so in this way our traditional paths and living journeys would be renewed and filled again with hope and purpose.

The understanding that the Creator is not just the Hebrew or the Christian god: but the creative and guiding force of all of our souls in

## Carrying the Chalice Forward

our journeys together through life; that we gain access to through our own prayers and sacred practices. These beliefs are equally supported by the inner circle teachings of most religions and spiritual sects from around the world. The journey within: whether we follow the moon road, or the path of the sun across the sky or the Stations of the Cross has always been to join in silence with the heart of creation to allow the gifts to rise up and be shared with ourselves or with the rest of creation. Sitting in silence and listening to our gifts as they rise from the centre of creation, from within each of us, is even at the heart of the teachings of many of the ancient and modern spiritual movements. Gaining the indigenous roads, without falling prey to the dogmatic slanders of the commercial needs for survival and conquest, requires that we honour the truth of what it means to be indigenous. By being true grandchildren of the Creator, our commitment is to hold all of creation firmly in our heart using our greater mind as our conscience. In loving ourselves and accepting the love that flows from the Creator, for who and what we are as human beings, is the accepting of our own true inheritance and connection to the original ancient formative source of life.

One of the basic teachings of our elders is that: as we share our gifts we gain the potential to receive greater gifts ourselves; because we are freely sharing the heart of creation with one

# Carrying the Chalice Forward

another. This tradition has been continually experienced from the start of the papal supported incursions to the new world by all visitors and allies. The indigenous heart of the Americas has always been lovingly open to sharing and giving from what the creator has freely shared with us. It is only human of us to expect the same kindness in return. We still hold out that hope.

When we view the evolution of our worldwide family as human beings, the loss of our collective families could be viewed as one of our darker hours. Our hope is that through the honouring and remembering of who and what we are today, as part of the continuation of our ageless journey as a family, we are bringing light to the truth of our own eternal existence and purpose. In this way our ancestors are able to live in and through us today by our bringing their living consciousness back into the world.

As our own families strove to approach life as a sacred and holy gift; and embraced the mergers with the families from Europe as part of our ongoing indigenous tradition, a great potential was born. As we, the Bois Brule, today continue our long-held path of viewing all people as sacred and worthy of love and protection, we carry forward the sacredness of these traditions. Our ways of sharing and embracing all of our families as sacred carries forward our maternal indigenous teachings as

## Carrying the Chalice Forward

a light for the rest of the families to follow today. Sharing our truth and our light is really all we can offer each other in helping to regain our paths, while fulfilling our needs and desires for community and love. Knowing and walking in the shoes of our ancestors, with light and love, helps to regain that potential for all of creation — and especially humanity.

The truth of our understanding is that the enemy is within each of us. Whether we choose light or dark as our message to the world: it is of our own choosing. Following the dogmatic path of rightness over love is a simple mistake each of us is eternally capable of. It is what the small mind, or our ego, constantly tricks us into doing. Returning to our own sacred light is a choice we may each freely make. Shining our radiance from within our own heart is our endless birthright, and our continuous potential gift to each other. Surrendering to this truth from within, will free us from the small minds, release our troubled souls; and bring us to the consciousness of healing from which we can each fully embrace and help change the world forever.

## *I let go of Paradise*

I let go of paradise
I free myself from the pain
I enter the light of my soul

# Carrying the Chalice Forward

**I SCREAM**

I free myself from the darkness
I open my heart to the pain
I feel it all I let it go
I feel it all I let it go
I regain my strength and I go on

Yah nah hah nah heh
Yah nah hah nah heh
Yah nah hah nah heh
Heya

I accept that it was only fear
that kept me in chains
in my need for salvation

I let go of paradise
I free myself from the pain
I enter the light of my soul
**I SCREAM**

I mourn the good times
I feel the rain
I release the dream
I free my soul
**I SCREAM**

I let go of paradise
I free myself from the pain
I enter the light of my soul
**I SCREAM**
**I SCREAM AGAIN**

# Carrying the Chalice Forward

I accept the tenderness I am offered
I trust in the peace of the night
I face the darkness in my rage

I let go of paradise
I free myself from the pain
I enter the light of my soul
**I SCREAM**

I release my agendas of fear
I speak clearly from my soul
my way in is my way out

Yah nah hah nah heh
Yah nah hah nah heh
Yah nah hah nah heh

I let go of paradise
I free myself from the pain
I enter the light of my soul
**I SCREAM**

I learn from the sparrow in the cage
I set myself free
I don't ask why
I just go

Yah nah hah nah heh
Yah nah hah nah heh
Yah nah hah nah heh

Heya

# 9

*Carrying the Chalice Forward*

# 9

# _Carrying the Chalice Forward_

The dream is the cup of our freedom pouring onto the fires set by our nightmares while we were asleep. Waking up to the dream restores our freedom to the cup of our own true imagining. Sharing the dream as we share the cup awakens the fire in all the sleepers. Coming home to the waking dream is our tribute to life everlasting and to the fulfilling of our duty to live the dream today.

The hope we have is that, through sharing the understandings of our origins, we will help inspire the families from around the world to arise and take up their full inherent responsibilities for fulfilling their sacred and holy purpose for all life.

**Carrying the Chalice Forward**

Although it may not be apparent at first, through following the purpose of Pharaoh's dream we can learn to each regain our part of

# Carrying the Chalice Forward

the human/divine consciousness left behind in our haste as children.

Our living journey is really just agreeing to enter the ever-present and all-encompassing silence of our own souls, to attain ascension through consciously joining with the Great Mind. In the centre of this great mind we are forever united with the heart of creation interwoven into the fabric of the universe as the Great Laws of Peace. In this silence is where we are always clean in our thoughts and will, and our attainment of peace can endure for eternity.

All who ascend the steps of peace endure the fire of our own soul's dissension, through its desire to enter the physical world. We are each capable of knowing we came here to experience the physical; yet, hopefully wise enough, not to be bound by its insolence and depravity. Our steps for our own lives are clear, as they were formed in the imagining and creation of our own journey. Our individual collections of songs and teachings drawn from the centre of our own souls are here to guide and provide comfort for ourselves and others on our journeys. By mastering the physical demands and needs of survival, and surrendering our will to the attainment of peace; and the willing creation of a balance with nature that is in harmony with life and creation, supporting our families living together in gentle tender love

## Carrying the Chalice Forward

and beauty, we embrace the full magnificence of love.

One hope we have, is that in striving to rediscover the truth of our human family we are then each free to choose to walk together on this road as a family. While we may not all agree on the points we each discern, and some topics may become more personally relevant than many of us have yet dreamed of, the untold reality is that we are each capable of approaching these discussions in a spirit of togetherness. With a combined hope of the potential of restoring our inter-connections as a family, many may emerge from the depths of their own research with miraculous discoveries and renewed wonder at our true inter-connectedness. It is our belief that, as a worldwide noble and indigenous family, we carry the full strength to begin the work of healing many of the false perceptions still rampant in the body of the world today.

By choosing to lance the bilious creations spawned by previous versions of writers of history, we are moving to take our place as warriors on the front line of a very old battle. Our families, from the four corners of the world, will be able to come forth to help re-interpret the facts and to help write and publish stories closer to the truth—that are no longer just bedtime stories. The ongoing efforts to create open and free exchanges of infor-

## Carrying the Chalice Forward

mation will hopefully inspire the honesty of researchers, and lovers of more truthful reading, for generations to come. Our eternal descendants may then be free to hold high their heads, and unveil their true identities; and gain strength in the humbling knowledge of having survived the ordeals and trials which many of our families underwent. Fully piercing the veils of illusion around what it means to be Sovereign will be the least of our accomplishments for the future.

When all is said and done, though, we would hope that we are able to take the important steps toward finding a peaceful way through the poison that flows from the wounds created by the lies of the past, and the mistaken and false beliefs. Building a bridge of peace over this river of misplaced ideals is like calling a truce between the fans of rival soccer teams in the sudden death finale. Even wading through the river of the dead, and returning, seems a somewhat easier task than one of making peace with people when truth is such a long-forgotten commodity. The hopes, lies and denials that have gone into creating so many different versions of the new world, most of which were based on hiding the origins of what came before, must all be somehow atoned for and reparations made in order for our soul-based journeys as a human family to move forward, and for all people to willingly walk together as family.

# Carrying the Chalice Forward

By attempting to bury, in words and deceit, those who opposed the fabrication of the biased and imagine-less stories like Columbus; the propaganda machines had to work overtime to make their own stories even somewhat credible. Yet, relying on the timidity and tolerance of the subjugated dependants, and of the born again new-world mind set, little effort was required: because everyone was easily enticed with the offers of receiving their own benefits, including the land to build their own castles on and the opportunities to become rich. As we all need to survive, it is quite easy for many of us to understand how we could get caught up in this game; yet, beyond survival, we are entirely capable of reaching for the pinnacle of human ingenuity: to make peace our focus for achievement and our unending gift to the world. All we really have to do is come clean and tell the truth.

When we take a step back and consider actually what types of people many are forced into becoming, through living under the bureaucratic system, currently sponsored by the churches and the commercial powers; our answers can be quite humbling. Depending on which side of the fences we sit can determine whether we are aware of the harm being done to the balance of life on the earth or whether we are asleep or unconscious. Reflecting on: What type of human beings do we want to become? What do we want our descendants to

## Carrying the Chalice Forward

think about what we have done? — And all we haven't done? Provides the urgency to answer the question of: Do we want to remain asleep in our subservience for eternity or do we wish to bring honour to the beauty of our own creations and live lives of light, honesty and dignity?

The impact on the consciousness of the western lands, as promoted through the media and propaganda machines, about the natural world being easily manageable and survivable; is underhandedly giving permission for the ongoing destruction of the earth to still continue. This same underhanded approach is similar to the one the recent pope took in saying it was time to eliminate the rest of Hellenistic thought. The fact that we play these games, while sitting back and watching the total destruction of the planet, shows how little consciousness we actually are able to use in our own lives. The wisdom speakers like Suziki, Black Elk and others have shown that it is only in our minds and consciousness that destruction begins when we allow our egos to have the final say. Bureaucracy and religion require our inner surrender to their small-minded agendas: so that we can be controlled and so that their empires are expanded and moved forward. By refocusing our soul's inner power, our great mind is then accessible to our consciousness; and the forces of creation begin to work with our every thought and action.

# Carrying the Chalice Forward

With these forces at our beck and call we are able to regain our own living power of choice; and can change the direction of the world from towards destruction to towards the enhancement, benefit and balance of all life.

The agendas, and constant desires of the bureaucratic mind, are to silence the conscience of our minds and hearts and have us subjugate our soul's journey to the irresponsible will of blind obedience. Money, and the management of money, can brook no opposition from the caring and loving nature of our hearts. Commerce without conscience, and the pursuit of unlimited expansion; unbalanced to the needs of the earth, are the products of the small-minded egos bent only on the agendas of the few who control and manage the flow of their currencies. The teaching and living of the Great Mind enhances everyone's potential through helping each of us overcome the taught subservience to the unconscious, commercial economy; and through holding onto our inherent and full sacred responsibilities for all life. By holding to the sacred balance of life through responsibly contributing to the return to harmony and balance of life, we become stronger human beings. By allowing for the caring and nurturing requirements of the earth to be delivered and administered through sharing our power, and helping keep all life safe and in harmony with our own original sacred

## Carrying the Chalice Forward

journeys, we each step closer to the heart of the Creator.

Our inactions to the known injustices of the world are a form of consent that needs to be urgently overcome. Our souls need to be inspired to action. Just as many of the leaders of the world have failed to respond to the atrocities dealt towards our indigenous families over the last 500 years, in all parts of the world, we need to rise up our consciousness to spend the next thousand years reversing these tragedies that still affect our entire human family. We need every soul to be with us and support all of us on this journey; if we are to squeak through the eye of the needle now facing the entire human family — especially if we are to emerge as anything resembling a higher order of human being.

By refusing any longer to benefit from supporting the lies of the old propaganda machines, between what is termed the old world and the new world, we can put aside being the beneficiaries of these lies. Following endless years of ongoing oppression against our main families, and the more recent years against our indigenous families, the challenges of the past will not be easily forgotten. It may be that when we choose to make peace *more* than just a word to use when it is profitable to do so, is when we will be assured that there will always be a true haven for our descen-

## Carrying the Chalice Forward

dants. The faithful, true warriors speaking out against the lies behind the silence, in this growing age of peace and unbiased knowledge, will forever stand tall and be counted among the heroes and heroines of our age.

Beyond peace, though, we believe it is ultimately important for all people to remember their own inherent responsibility for all life; and to continue to uphold the sacred balance by caring for, and nurturing, a way of living in harmony with all of creation. In so doing, a harmonious balance is created within ourselves and extends into the rest of creation. Agreeing to silence the old world beliefs of dominance and subjugation, spawned through using racial segregation and political superiority, we can then choose to create a new world: where we are each capable of remaining committed to the voices of acceptance and cooperation; thereby inspiring racial tolerance and acceptance; thereby enhancing the true potential for long-lasting peace and the general prosperity for all people and life the world over. Easily said, yet this remains our lifelong challenge and daily need.

One of the sad realities is that, all through our histories, many of our own families were involved on both sides of the fence; plagued with the same unending needs for land and revenue. Many had had to sit on both sides and took part in many harsh games just

# Carrying the Chalice Forward

because of their needs to survive. Many of these descendants are now waking up to the new choices we currently have: for the fulfilling of our elders' and ancestors' dreams; and for living our visions and hopes for a peaceful, heaven-formed future. Many of our Bois Brule and other families, from all parts of the world, are being drawn forward by the remembering of their vows of allegiance; and seem to, for the most part, have managed to keep portions of their ongoing commitment to peace, gentleness and love for their worldwide family alive. Beyond the past though, and our ongoing needs for food, clothing and shelter; our higher needs for community and expressing the truth of our soul's heartfelt expressions, will urge us ever towards the true peace inherent within the beauty and joy of family. Our own desires to right the wrongs will move us ever onwards towards creating the community we each continually crave from the heart of our souls.

When we can gather from all over the world and discuss the belief-shattering subjects such as: peace, love and forgiveness; as early pre-Templar families did in their travels and settlements, we can then emerge with a more complete vision for the future. The biggest hurdle to discussing peace today: is the surrender of all that which has been gained through the deceit and lies of past endeavours, however rightly subscribed. The legal titles

## Carrying the Chalice Forward

claimed, the use of inappropriate feudal laws within foreign territories, the legislations used to create false trails of legal precedence, the ignoring of and cabalistic approach to chasing the true custodians of the land away, the changing of indigenous traditions to match the non-indigenous outcome desired by the negotiators and, basically all the outright lies and deceit will all have to be surrendered and accounted for. The discussion of all these issues will of necessity be done with all of the families involved, and equally represented, for any resolution or peace to be permanently achieved.

The quiet commitment to peace and the timeless pledges of hope for the future; may be discerned through viewing the efforts of our family in the co-creation, funding and building of the city of Montreal. With committed souls like Martin Olivier, Jeanne Manse, the master architect mason D'Alleboust and others; many ongoing alliances and endeavours were indelibly entrenched with the Algonquin and other families. These alliances are highlighted in our memories as a dream worthy of being fulfilled. During the colonial French incursions into our territories when King Louis sent Hector Calliere to help solidify the peace between our families; close to 100 indigenous tribes united in forming the Great Peace of 1701. The main combined indigenous families at that time stretched over the trade routes of

## Carrying the Chalice Forward

the entire eastern seaboard, the Louisiana territories, onto the Great Plains, and into the north. Roughly including up to 3/4ths of all the trading-based indigenous families from the territories of the east, west, south and north of the continent; these alliances built permanent roads of peace to all the indigenous families. The elements of peace that remain woven within the bounds of our families' alliances, inspired with the memories of our ancestor's dreams, will hopefully help carry us forward to fulfill the true potential of peace for humanity on the earth; and help to carry us out into the stars of the world today as a united family.

Our families include the living proof of how the Northmen (Vikings), the Cistercians, Goths and others are known to have travelled, settled and traded in the new world long before Columbus. The families under the sponsorship of people like Prince Henry Sinclair and others, whose descendants are known to have built long-standing memorials, including Rosslyn Chapel, the Newport Tower and other markers, hold a different lamp for guidance than those who came later. Life can become a much easier road to travel when we declare, for each other; that we agree and remain committed to living peacefully and honourably together, the world over. Knowing a bit more of the truth by exploring documents, and doing research to support the true stories, is

# Carrying the Chalice Forward

helping to bring the return of these great-minded and good-hearted values, and hopefully the return of our families to living in a permanent state of peace, love, joy and harmony together.

These early Temple-based Masonic families acted differently than the perfidious behaviour of many of their brothers in the newer country lodges, who were often led astray in their desires for building self-serving empires. Through dis-regarding the true alliances held and born into the blood bonds of our real families, these later masons missed the true points of forming the brotherhood. The changes in the lodges are known and remembered, by and through our family; yet most of the current adherents are actually innocent and lack much knowledge of the betrayals that have coloured the past four hundred years. With a return to foundations of the true brotherhood, and the returning of the balance towards stewardship and compassion; the removal of the aegis of the small-minded will allow us to then begin to rebuild the function of our true family's purpose achieved only through mutually joining in alliance with all of the real indigenous families of the earth. We can then make true choices to live our full responsibilities for all of our actions, and faithfully and dutifully impact the earth with beauty and magnificence; as true brothers and

# Carrying the Chalice Forward

sisters in the league as guardians of the balance of life on earth and in the universe.

This is not to say we have to camp out on each other's back porch—yet, even that holds some promise; however, it is of importance that we each continue to stay in touch as family, carrying our combined knowledge and teachings forward. Peace can only begin within each of us as we begin to remember what the Creator gave to us and begin to do what jobs each of us has to accomplish in our journeys within creation. The current collective job for many: being the rewriting of the status quo. Our joy should hopefully include the extra benefit of experiencing how to live together in peace; so that all of our cousin clans and families, from around the world, can remember how to further the art of making plows and shovels from the discarded tools of war.

The one true thing we know for certain about the past is: that lies had to be told. Our hidden lies were held in our silence; both for our survival, and for creating a haven for the great-minded and true-hearted to live together in peace and prosperity. The other lies were part of the human equation, designed to allow greed and self-serving conquest to serve the fools of the ego. Greater lies have been told, all in the name of what is good for us, yet the Creator guides the resolution of all these paths

# Carrying the Chalice Forward

to serve the visions of the true families. It is now the time to reverse the lies and to retell the true stories of our journeys, within the new and the old worlds.

The chalice is really the cup of peace we offer to all families to drink of our blood as allies; united in this beautiful creation world, in love and joy together. All those who drink willingly from this cup are the true peoples of the Creator. The rest, although innocent, are stuck living with their small-minded approach to the world and will likely spend their lives craving what it is they have only to open their minds and hearts to embrace. The chalice is eternally open to all who behold their own innocence, in the magnificence of their enjoined dreams of peace, flowing from the miraculous wonder and beauty of creation. Our hearts hold the blood bond of our joining in the dream we continue to still co-create with each other, in this community of life; without boundaries or limitations. The heart of the land, and spirit of the Americas, calls to the true spirits and hearts of those whose higher thoughts are to no longer ravage her; but to find gentler and less intrusive means to survive and live together on the earth. Through honouring our relationship to the earth, bound with the blood of the true families to the heart of the indigenous world; we can then awaken to our true conscience; and know that peace is the ultimate goal; and

# Carrying the Chalice Forward

sharing, the only means of rightful acquiescence to love.

In working to rewrite our collective history on these shores, we have been able to gain some insight and inspiration from an old public school history of England and Canada, as authorized by the Education Department of Ontario in 1885. In the preamble to the text, the editors emphasize that... "history is just a story and this is just our version of it." These vivid and self glorifying terms of reference have provided us with some useful and ongoing guidelines to search out the seeds of our own family's story, in this, and other written material. Learning to also balance the emerging events and their myths, with current archaeological and historical evidence, has brought our resulting version to be a little less tainted and a lot more humane. Rewriting the stories of the Bois Brule/Metis, as they are tied to the origins of the countries in which we currently live, is a pivotal point of understanding the true origins of the real people; and the true forces fuelling the beliefs in the inherent rights to freedom and self expression. Although never a complete telling of the true story, we sincerely hope it will be one that brings some joy, happiness and relief to our familial descendants and supporters.

At the time of the open exchanges of discovery, Amerindian and European families had been evolving almost separately for such a long period of time that they considered themselves to be of different races. The Amerindian looked with disdain, for the most part, on the lack of ability or natural skills to survive; of the newcomers. Yet, with some of the first mixed blood offspring, the potential for benefit was visible in their obvious increased strength and capabilities. Many families at that time made overtures and requests to formally ally their main families through marriage unions. When it was discovered that these new offspring could be trained in the indigenous traditions for survival, and were able to learn the indigenous languages; the doors to heaven, and survival, for the newcomers were opened: and the positions of their offspring, as peacekeepers, and as emissaries of goodwill for the trade and family alliances, was forever assured.

By merging the different peoples to form new peoples: as our grandmothers, and as Odin himself had taught in the old stories; we now scientifically understand that this is how our old families knew how to build a stronger DNA and invite more potential to always help overcome future obstacles. Through the arranged intermarriages of the main indigenous sacred, holy and leading families with the sacred, noble and old bloodlines of the visiting families; the emerging mixed-blood race of people actually get to inherit the noble

## Carrying the Chalice Forward

and sacred responsibilities for both parent groups. In our case, these unions in a short period of time had grown to include most of the old families for the majority of the world. What these families do with that nobility and that knowledge, has in the past, and will undoubtedly help shape the future of all humanity. Whether we are the ancient powerful, all-seeing guides capable of leading all mankind forward; will most likely depend on whether we wear our hundred dollar suit or jeans and a t-shirt. Already, though, the changes brought about through these permanent unions have changed the course of the development of the world more than most writers would care to admit.

Our blood is strong. It has strengthened the blood of all indigenous nations and been strengthened in return. The young, now coming forward, seem ready to bring true justice and prosperity to the world.

Most indigenous people within the next generation, or so, may come to fully know their own obligations and responsibilities to become better acquainted with their own traditional family ties through the Bois Brule. What the Creator's timeless purpose was, and is, for creating the union of these families from such a tumultuous past; can only, as far as we believe, be for the whole world's benefit and glory. The descendants of these mergers are the

# Carrying the Chalice Forward

fulfillment of the old traditional teachings from both families of origin and have a great part to play in the final outcome of the history being born today.

To honour who we are as indigenous people today, we are taught to give honour and place to all of our ancestors, even those who are white. With grace, we can extend the arm of forgiveness into our own souls and reach back to our true connections with the Creator in our heart; and bring forth the light that shines from our own innocence. We trust that the shining of this light from the heart of our souls, in unison with each other, will open pathways through any dark or turbulent times ahead. Our traditional seers remind us that very soon each of us may come to understand the trick the Creator has played on us all. One of our true teachings is that when we catch ourselves laughing at the joke being played on us, we have then reached the truth and innocence of all things. When we have the courage to ask: "What is it that we truly believe?" and "Can our blond grandchildren really be the Indians we thought they would be?" We will know we have travelled a great distance and likely will still be laying on the ground laughing.

In this curious age we can often find ourselves looking for help both from the past and from the future. When, as children, we ask the Creator to make us king, or queen, and hope

## Carrying the Chalice Forward

for that day to arrive; the Creator sits back and laughingly, yet quietly, waits while we slowly unravel the mystery: only to discover that there are many kings and queens born into the world today. When we discover that what is asked of us: is our taking action on the responsibility of already being what we ask for, we can then join in the laughter with the rest of creation. The divine breath we have all been given, which has guided our footsteps into our separate havens and kept the holy seeds alive, has been part of each of our own private histories. Yet, we are all here together to enter into the consciousness of our true beings. What will we do as the immortal kings and queens of the world? and of heaven? Will we be for peace or will we demand retribution for the wrongs committed in our names? Will we take up our responsibilities? and usher in the age of peace to last for the remainder of time? What do our hearts, and our bloodline, compel us to do?

When asking these questions about our own family's journey, the answer received was to bring our families together to enter into a blanket alliance, formalizing the union of our families, by traditionally rebinding our families together. This action would help lay the groundwork for future discussions of peace. The indigenous teaching of returning to the blanket is of the same purpose as asking for forgiveness of everyone, and retying our

# Carrying the Chalice Forward

bundles together; in order to regain the connections to the dreams and hopes of our ancestors. Weaving each of our families' hopes for peace into a blanket alliance, founded on our acceptance of each other as free people, is the fulfilling of our vision to help re-unite our dreams with the true vision the Creator holds for all of us as his people.

Through agreeing to hold the earth as sacred, and by setting aside territories for all of our families to live on; as well as for camping and visiting, in regions where our safety and protection are secured; we can begin this journey together to reunite the hopes of our ancestors and re-envision the true dreams for a new world that can include the fullness and potential of all our indigenous families.

**The Blanket Alliance**

Beginning at the heart and joining each new family in a woven pattern spiralling outward in a braided blanket, all of the families shall abide together as allies forever. The blankets will be gathered from the four corners of the world and joined at the heart, binding all indigenous families together as one family holding the earth and all people as sacred.

The one true thing about the indigenous version of history is that we have all had to

# Carrying the Chalice Forward

hide from parts of our histories that were true, in order to stay alive and carry on. Mistakes have been made by all peoples of the world since the beginning of time. Being indigenous does not make us any better, yet it does give us a better chance at being honest about our connection to the earth. Each member of an indigenous family is capable of letting their small mind take them away from the truth. We can each now chose to back each other up or let the chips fall where they may. Our hope is that we will back each other up: for the truth of our shared responsibility for the harmony and balance of all life; and the safe-guarding of our mother the earth from any further destruction.

What do we do now as we begin to remember that we are each sovereign and free? Do we make and support peace? Or do we tear the world apart? Our hope is that the love in our hearts and souls is strong enough to carry us beyond our own childish reactions to the events of the world; and allow us all to return to the same table we have met at previously, over the ages. Our united family's truth is that only by surrendering our own agendas, and entering in freely to bind ourselves again with our families, will we find a space of equality: sheltered by the pillars of faith, hope, love and charity—or, as some families refer to them, surprise, encouragement, empathy and peace.

# Carrying the Chalice Forward

## **Carrying the Chalice forward**

Carrying the Chalice forward
In times of hard
Where ships lay barred
And friendly sails grounded
There lived a bard
With fists of steel
And wings of gold
Who never ever faltered
Quite right you say
T'is never to play
In this world of the half hearted
Through boon 'n bust
With nary a post
Or a lift of a cheer
We humble and mar
And sit in the car
Our huddle bubble
Where right you will sway
Under the bar away
Atop this here middle
With a bump 'n a nod
'N a swirl 'n a turtle
A drop this hear faux pas

# Carrying the Chalice Forward

With kings on the run
From a child with a gun
We hid under a little
Now pop we may
'N jigger 'n poke
'N jimmy a side to the middle
Two steps we hope
'N many a twirl and a shade
Afore the sun gets to noon
'N the pope gets a bidd'le
'Ere we stride our long bows
'N stroke our long arms
Abreast our dear muddle
knee deep in a puddle
we splash 'n we wain
a good herd of earth
astride his wee 'lass
all tumble 'n mirth
a galloping, galloping gallop
the crown to bear
atop our fair hair
with ruby in the middle
her host to us sway
and many divers stay
cherish the ground 'n the knight

# Carrying the Chalice Forward

> pointing the way to hither gone
> 'n staying the course of light
> around to our gathering we stay
> a bright horse all painted in grey
> ending night 'n bringing day
> a feather to brush a way
> the cobwebs in our heart.

If we take the example of the Great Peace of 1701, or even the works of our Norman and Celtic ancestors, and compare these to the Great Land Grabs a mere century later; we are able to view some very harsh and disparaging activities. It would seem that the commercial fight for the economic boon through domination of the new world (and the old), is not overly different from that which was faced during the early beginnings of the Roman empirical bureaucracies. History shows us so easily that the tools of war are not always metal, that they are quite often merely the words we use and rely on for our self expression and in describing who and what we are.

One understanding is that the real gifts that were and are available in coming to the new world; are the long histories and teachings of the different peacemakers. Whether it is White Buffalo Calf-robe Woman from the Blackfoot,

# Carrying the Chalice Forward

Deganawideh of the Ongwaonwe, or other Coyotes, Chickadees, Woodpeckers, twins or teachers of other families; the common threads uniting these teachings flow from a similar spirit of reaching for something beyond our own limited human perception. Unfortunately, these teachings continue to elude many that still place an over reliance on warfare for profit and survival. Breaking free of our need to use old or outmoded ways of brute force, and hidden agendas, will hopefully allow the true spirit of family to rise from the soil; giving us our new inspiration by adding wisdom and compassion to our every thought and deed. Through listening to the truth of the teachings and knowledge of the real peacekeepers: we will hopefully gain the much needed guidance to face the pending situations rising up as the earth, and the people, recoil and rebel at the overtaxing of freedom and resources from the four corners of the earth.

The original teachers and role models through which our Bois Brule families descend all brought with them traditions of peace and faithful adherence to higher civilized traditions; that supported and acknowledged the benefit, and purpose, of true peace. The inherent wisdom of forming permanent peaceful alliances that stem from the full indigenous traditions was handed through both the matriarchs and patriarchs of our families. Our mothers and grandmothers

# Carrying the Chalice Forward

brought us their traditions and teachings and their ways of living in the wild. They also taught us our roles as emissaries and how to live with and share the territories with other races and cultures. Carrying this knowledge forward is our inherent and essential responsibility; especially today, in helping urgently restore some of the balance and harmony to the natural world and to our families and cousins.

The cross-cultural teachings and regional based trade languages our families created, and used for trading and communicating, combined with the Norman French spoken by the early traders, created an interesting tapestry of perspective and values. Our combined languages of the Ouendat, Cree, Algonquin, Creek, Blackfoot, M'ikM'ak, Abenaqui, Shawnee, Lakota, Assiniboine, Dakota, Chippewa, Sarcee, Creek, Ojibwa, Dene and others merged easily with the Norman French words creating full new languages and regional forms of patois for communicating. The bloodlines, responsibilities and traditions of the speakers of these languages, for the most part, were combined and retained by those speakers who often remained living near, or stayed connected to, their original indigenous territory and families. These families today still hold reciprocal responsibilities to their cousin clans and families; with blood-based traditions impelling

# Carrying the Chalice Forward

each of us to deal honourably, respectfully and reciprocally with our cousins; and to expect the same in return. Ignoring these traditions, and holding anything less is a step towards the declaration of war and a breech of full indigenous tradition.

Our own family's bloodlines stem into the Outriouendat (Wendat), Arendakohi (Huron), Dene, Cree, Ojibwa, Chippewa, Saulteaux, Abenaki, M'icMaq, Nipissing, Algonquin, Iroquoian, Mascouten, and many others just known as Amerindian. Our visiting noble family bloodlines include the original crowns of England, Jerusalem, Portugal, Spain, Ireland, France, Rome, Scotland, Italy, Navarre, Norway, and many more. As we honour and hold our responsibilities to our cousin families, they are free to honour and hold the same equal responsibilities to us; especially in the acknowledging of our shared rights of life and liberty, and our equally true worldwide inheritance as free people. Our combined family's rights to exist and live within the territories on Turtle Island, as well as almost anywhere else on the earth, stem from our own shared bloodlines which bind us equally with the heads of all the indigenous families, and the old world noble families, as equal descendants. We have each walked the same path of descent; and the same noble and sacred inheritances are shared. As the main trading families for the last several hundred years, our

# Carrying the Chalice Forward

interconnections and blood ties hold us in eternal union with the majority of all of the main families. We are the descendants of the bonds of peace, love and friendship; entered into by our ancestors with full knowledge of the forming of blood alliances. Our inherent responsibilities are to continue to honour these alliances and carry these pledges of peace to our families and allies from all the four corners of the earth.

It is our path to understanding, and the way we have learned, to search for and explain that which is within us and known to be true. The Metis Bois Brule/Metis (Otipemesiuk) are 100% indigenous as inherited through our mothers and grandmothers and our fathers and grandfathers of full indigenous origin. We are their full-blood offspring. Our tradition is that our full inheritance flows through both male and female so that all of our children are fully indigenous, noble and sacred. We are all equally responsible and free. Our families formed permanent bonds of peace based on the unending alliance of our full families. Our families and bloodlines are forever entwined as one.

What I have learned of our families is that the indigenous origins of our allied blood ties may also be referred to with the indigenous reference points of the white and black lands and families from across the Atlantic; who

# Carrying the Chalice Forward

were caught in an ancient blood feud and bureaucratic conflict over: who rules the afterlife, and who rules the rights and responsibilities for each family. As descendants of these head families from across the Atlantic and from Turtle Island, we share in these responsibilities. We also share the unique position and authority to speak with all nations as brothers and sisters: tied in blood and indigenous responsibility to all life and property on both sides of the Atlantic.

Our responsibility, as we understand it, is one based on love of all our families; yet we are also bound to the authority of blood and the inherent responsibility for the land and the souls within it and upon it. We are the first and the last families. We are from Adam and Noah, and we are from the twins. We are the children of Christ, Mohammed and Nape. We are the Creator's children who are waking from our dreams to embrace the love of all living beings; and we still hold the authority to bring all life to the same table to discuss peace on terms which value life and love, without regard for agendas or mandates. We are the spiritual possessors of the true teachings of the descendants of Pharaoh, Caesar, Horus, Zeus, Odin, Ra, Quetzalcoatl, Coyote, the Peacemaker, the war chiefs, the tricksters, Oldman and so on and on.

# Carrying the Chalice Forward

It is our job to work out a solution to the darkness that currently engulfs the whole wide world as a result of the selfish endeavours of unbridled commercial exploitation and democratic mob rule; that continues to act irresponsibly towards the environment and the forces which support all life for eternity. We must maintain this balance of male and female; to commit to holding the darkness away from impacting the ability of the forces of life to continue in harmony. Our aim and our goal are to provide the dream for humanity to follow to reach the full benefit of creative magnificence. Our responsibilities are to bring our journey full circle to invite all of our connected families to the same table of peaceful joining so that these life forces may encourage us on the path for good into the future. Anything less, as we know in our souls, will be the destruction of life and the end of humanity as a positive force for good. Only in harmony with man and woman, in sacred balance with the forces of creation and beauty, and power, and magnificence, and hope; do we retain or hold any of our potential for extending the gifts of faith, hope, charity and love.

Living and being together as a family is truly the only option that engenders any form of lasting peace. It will only be by building on the dreams of the original peacemakers, that we are able to renew the potential to enhance the full quality of life. Only then will we be able

# Carrying the Chalice Forward

to stop agreeing to exterminate ourselves. Being part of the active solution to the ills of the world, we then get to laugh at the mistakes of others (and maybe ourselves, too), and rise above our smallness to the greatness we are each born to.

Humour has always been both a great diffuser and healer of our families. It may never be that we come fully to love one another, yet we may still get to laugh and share some quality time together. It is through this common sharing of laughter, and openly meeting to discuss our hearts and minds, that love remains the only true hero of our time.

We must remember that the origin of peace does not start in the middle of a war. Peace only starts when we first lay down our weapons and surrender to the love in our souls for all life, and for one another. When we stop and think of our mother the earth, first; we can then freely carry her beauty forward. Through embracing and living the full responsibility inherent in being truly sovereign we can emerge from the chrysalis of sleep into walking our true paths and destiny. It is in beginning from a spirit of peace that we are more likely to continue in peace, providing much benefit to future generations, and uniting our families together again in lasting peace.

On that note, let us begin, in peace, with our

# Carrying the Chalice Forward

true cousins and family, by joining hands across the Atlantic to bring one another back together into an allied circle of family, united in walking this path of peace together. What we learn and discuss will undoubtedly shatter the illusions of the world and lay the seeds of renewal for all beings of truth for eternity.

FAMILY RESEARCH AND STUDY PROJECTS

Researching the origins of some of our families, championed by individuals from the Sinclair, St. Clair and other families, has brought us a much more comprehensive view of history compared with what has normally been allowed to be published. Carrying this research forward through the combined Archaeological, DNA, Linguistic and Cultural studies, we shall be easily able to amass the volume of verifiable content necessary to continue to rewrite history.

Like the petals of an unfolding rose, we will spread the scented leaves of our efforts to all the corners of the globe.

Comparing DNA results obtained thus far, with currently existing genealogical records, seems to have brought us forward in understanding a Nordic, as well as a mid-European and eastern, origin for many of our paternal families. The emerging viewpoint

## Carrying the Chalice Forward

from the research seems to be of a cohesive and select family group that has managed to stay together over many millennia. Tracking the movements of this family, from their far eastern sojourns; to their present hideaways, will likely keep researchers busy for many years to come. The major findings within many of the bloodlines are compared to, and often supported by, the shared oral and linguistic histories. Although not final, the emerging picture can be seen to support the experience of peaceful co-habitation through the merging and strengthening of certain families.

The matching of the Bois Brule/Metis family histories to our true histories; including the Valois, DeGuise and other royal or northern families, amoung others; will be championed through continuing the ongoing search for connections in all areas of current and future research. While the challenge of learning and exploring the possibility that the old world noble lines are now intrinsically bound to indigenous family lines of North and South America may upset a few tea carts, the ongoing discoveries give us some possibility of hope and comfort. What we do with the information, and how we act responsibly in knowing our full heritage, will shape much of the future to come. Learning to laugh and rejoice at the simplicity of our family's choices will quite possibly be our strong saving grace.

# Carrying the Chalice Forward

Some families of Bois Brule/Metis origin selected for special interest and study are Bourbon, Brabant, Latour, MacDougall, McDonald, Farquharson, Fraser, MacGillivray, Clare, Vallois, Nevarre, Bon, Godefroy, Baudouin, Gautier, Caille, Roger, Boucher, McGill, Bernard, Mauger (Maugis), Pepin, Cabot, Bousquet, Coulombe, David, Hamelin, Denis, Hugue, Auger, Templair, Clairoux, Edeline, Favel, Halle, Canada, Tanner, Brun, Harel, Laurin, LeBlanc, Lenoir, Chevalier, Poussin, the Saints..., Thierry, Stuart, Villiers, Vincent, Vivier, L'Esperance, Foi, Charite, Payne, LaHaye, Pitre, Ptolomee, Charron, Adam, McTavish, Thane, Hall, Zastre, Gervais, Roy, Chouard, Stuart, Grenier, Joseph, LeMadeleine, Messier, Blouf, Lalonde, Landry and many others.


A curious part of our collective Bois Brule/Metis history includes the tradition of the naming of our children after conquerors, Kings and Queens; many of whom represented certain aspects of change in the old world. In this way, names like Napoleon, Frederick, Isabella, Elizabeth, Edward, Auldijo, and others, continue with our families still. Even after Napoleon sold our American homeland, resulting in our expulsion and dispersal—and in some cases our total absorption—we continue to give honour to the name by still carrying it forward. Napoleon's descendants

## Carrying the Chalice Forward

are our family's cousins and they seem to have continued to marry into our extended families for several generations. In addition, we still maintain an extensive kinship and inter-marriage tradition with virtually all other noble families around the world.

Different parts of our stories include several main events from family members in places like Brazil, across the continent and elsewhere. These include stories of helping in the freeing of slaves; of saving the buffalo herds, of locally certain families uniting to break coercive monopolies and dominions, of finding and forming healing shrines and places of miracles. The mapping and charting of our shared homeland of North America was done long before Lewis and Clark. If it were not for the sharing of our maps with them, they would still be lost in the mountains today. Even the defense provided by our families against the aggressions of our southern neighbours, in search of their own stars, is why there is still a Canada today. The sacred healing events and teachings of many of our families have created a tapestry of shrines and grottos from one coast to the other.

The stories of the Lords and Ladies of the Plains, and the songs of the Bois Brule/Metis spiriting away the Dauphin to live with them on the Plains, still enchant us today. The stories of our sending a white Stallion to Mussolini

# Carrying the Chalice Forward

when he first gained power is just one of the highlights we still try to recall for our children. The stories of Gaultier de La Verendrye's Algonquin great uncles (whose birth name is Saguirou), helping lead the way west 40 years previous to him, and their descendants later being sought out and adopted by the Cree, are some of our own favourites.

For our own paternal history, the Carriere family is actually a direct paternal branch of the royal Caille family of Ireland who moved to France and Normandy supposedly to escape persecution. Branches of this family are known to include the lines of Sinclair, Godefroy, Baudouin, Callaway, O'Shea, Tanner and other notable families. Of later interest will be the comparison of studies tracking the old Kennedy, Smith, Johnson, Ford, Jefferson, Moore, Cook, Drake, Miller, Welsh, Frank, Forest, Bible, Luna, Cain, Fish, Salazar, Fork, Stone, Brown, Guthrie, Solomon, Roy, Rose, King, Laurans, Lottson and hundreds more whose origins seem to originate with one main family line. Many additional family lines go back through these early noble and royal families whose origins comprise virtually all of the modern Bois Brule/Metis family lines. It is no wonder the English got into a panic when, in the later 1800's, our families were approached by the Irish Fenian army to discuss a formal martial alliance. It may still be that these blood ties to Ireland will play a crucial

# Carrying the Chalice Forward

part in the restoring of the final balance needed to end the ongoing oppression against the free peoples of the world.

The understanding we have is that the expansion of this family into the regions of the Kingdoms of Heaven, England, France, Italy, Spain and elsewhere, including the new world, testifies to the true strength and indomitable spirit of Ireland. Our own branch was listed as coming over the waters to help Jeanne Manse, and company, with the defense and founding of Mount Royal and the building of the hospitals in Quebec and Montreal. Other stories are of our family line inter-woven in many other esoteric and fraternal histories, from the early Temple Masons and founders of the Blue Lodges to the Grand Masters for Upper and Lower Canada and other societies elsewhere. Our maternal lines go through the early allied unions of our families with our Micmac, Algonquin, Iroquoian and other cousins. Our own branch that came over to help with the building of Mount Royal eventually sprouted thousands of descendants taking root from one side of the country to the other.Our other family lines are interwoven in many other esoteric and fraternal histories from the early Temple Masons and founders of the Blue Lodges to the Grand Masters for Upper and Lower Canada and other societies elsewhere. Our maternal lines spread forth from their M'ikmaq, Algonquin, Iroquoian and

# Carrying the Chalice Forward

other origins to encompass virtually all of the indigenous families of North America.

Willing participants for the continuing research may join in through either or both the www.stclairresearch.com site and the Family Tree DNA site at www.ftdna.com under the Sinclair or Canadnat study groups.

The families interested in hosting their own initiatives to help heal the rifts of the past and bring health to the life of the earth may connect to the author through the publisher at St. Clair Publications. Allies and family groups are most certainly welcome to help with the studies and research activities; as well as to help reunite and reinvigorate the unending cause, and purpose, of our united families.

From the combined origins of our worldwide families—the Bahamas, Florida, the far north, the Great Plains, Eastern and Western North America and the south; to the Norman, Scotch, Flemish, Irish, Basque, Hebrew, Portuguese, Spanish, French and other family connections: we still hold a great potential for the dream of peaceful coexistence in harmony and love with all of life. Our combined family lines weave a very intricate and cohesive web, encompassing many of the old Masonic, engineering, artificer, Templar, Gnostic, noble, sacred and shamanic origins.

# Carrying the Chalice Forward

There also lies considerable humour in the fact that it was our old family that had conquered England in the eleventh century, setting the stage for this modern plague of propriety. The same modern royals, who often try so hard to show their lineages back to our own main families (those that even the smallest of our mixed-blood families take for granted), often forget to acknowledge us as their cousins — yet this is their choice. We are still here: and we do know who we are, and what our path is. As more families rejoin us in our journey, our growing strength as one true family; will hopefully encourage our diligence to live and expand the workings of peace to restore the living balance, and rights to life, for all of creation.

# Carrying the Chalice Forward

# 10

## *United Families*

# 10

## *United Families*

The following is a names list of many of our main families united through marriage with the early Temple Masonic, noble and chieftain families who chose to live together in peace as one family, merging their languages and traditions and becoming the Bois Brule/Metis root families. We follow both the paternal and maternal heritage, keeping us united with all of our families. Many of the indigenous spellings of names are absent, yet the known branches leading through each of the indigenous families are known and acknowledged. As we were formed in peace, our obligation is always for the truth of peace. Our maternal inheritance binds us to respond with love towards all of our family. Our paternal binds us to fulfill our responsibilities to the survival and prosperity of our families and of the land which nurtures us.

Our reason for providing the list of names is to share the depth of our research and our understandings of our known origins, and to allow families to find their points of connection behind the importance for writing these stories. There are several DNA studies

# Carrying the Chalice Forward

currently underway that may be of interest to many descendants hoping to balance their written histories with additional proofs and knowledge. Our hopes are to track the maternal and paternal lineages for all our various lineages to help correlate and compare the DNA findings with our own written and oral family histories.

**NAMES LIST**

Abram, Adam, Adams, Aden, Adennette, Adhemar, Africa, Agnier, Aguenier, Agenier, Aide, Aide-Crequi, Aiken, Ains, Ainsse, Aird, Allara, Allary, Allarie, Allie, Allard, Allary, Alscome, Amelin, Amiot, Amyot, Amyotte, Amler, Anderson, Angelique, Antil, Antill, Arcan, Arcand, Arcus, Arelle, Arlin, Arkneys, Armstrong, Arnoit, Arsineau, Asham, Aslin, Athanaise, Atkinson, Atryet, Attina, Aubert, Aubin, Aubichon, Auger, Auman, Aymont, Ayott, Ayotte, Azure,

Babie, Baby, Baubie, Bubbie, Badger, Baillarge, Bailly, Baillie, Baison, Ballendine, Ballenden, Balon, Balan, Banje, Baptiste, Barabe, Barbeau Baribeau, Barbou, Barckman, Baren, Baron, Barron, Bareille, Baril, Bargedin, Bargwain, Bariso, Bariteau, Barnabe, Barnard, Barnes, Barron, Bashe, Basin, Batillo, Baubien, Baubin, Baudouin, Bauvais, Bauvier, Beads, Bear, Beardy, Beaubien, Beauchamp, Beaucheman, Beauchemin, Beauchene, Beauchesne,

# Carrying the Chalice Forward

Beaudoin, Baudoin, Baudon, Baudeant, Beaudean, Beaudin, Beaudion, Beaudrie, Beaudria, Beaudry, Baudry, Beaudroin, Beaudwin, Beaugrand, Beaulieu, Beaupie, Beaupre, Beausoliel, Bejarge, Belan, Belanger, Belcour Belcourt, Bellecourt, Bele, Bellec, Beleque, Belisle, Belliveau, Bellaire, Belle, Bell, Belleau, Bellefeuille, Bellegarde, Belgarde, Belhumeur, Bellehumeur, Bellesoliel, Belliard, Bellival, Bender, Benerau, Benereau, Benic, Benneville, Benneau, Bennerman, Bennet, Benoit, Beniot, Benoist, Berard, Bercier, Bereau, Bureau, Berevin, Berger, Bergeron, Bergis, Beriault, Berisson, Berland, Breland, Bernard, Bernier, Berrard, Berthelet, Bertrand, Beseau, Beuton, Bibeau, Biencourt, Billiard, Billy, Bird, Birston, Bisset, Bisson, Bission, Biviret, Black, Blanc, Blanche Blanchette, Blayone, Blayon, Blayonne, Blain, Bleakley, Blette, Bleuve, Blondau, Blondeau, Blondin, Blandion, Blouf, Boarasa, Bourasa, Bourassa, Boardon, Bodette, Bohemier, Boicour, Boisclair, Boilard, Boileau, Boissonneau, Boisghulbert, Boisverd, Boisvert, Boivrun, Bolieu, Bolon, Bollen, Bond, Bondy, Bone, Bonhomme, Bonnault, Bonneau, Bonneville, Bosse, Bosset, Bottineau, Bouchard, Boucher, Boudreau, Boudri, Boudreau, Boudreault, Boudreaux, Boudril, Bouer, Bouin, Bowen, Boulton, Bourassa, Bourasseau, Brassa, Brosseau, Bourbon, Bourdeau, Bourdere, Bourdon, Bourgare, Bourgois, Bourgoise, Bourgeois, Bouret, Bourre, Bourret, Bourette, Bourier, Bourke, Bourque, Bousche, Bousquet,

# Carrying the Chalice Forward

Boutin, Bouton, Bouvet Bouvette, Bouvier, Boyden, Bowden, Boyer, Brabant, Breban, Briban, Bradaire, Braconnier, Brasconnier, Brasseau, Brazeau, Brault, Brough, Braux, Brauz, Brass, Brayant, Brazot, Breau, Brau, Breault, Breaux, Bredeur, Breland, Bremner, Bramner, Breyler, Brian, Brien, Briyen, Brisbe, Brisbo, Brisbois, Brisebois, Brisset, Brissette, Brown, Bruce, Brugere, Bruhler, Brulot, Brun, Brund, Bruneau, Brunet, Brunner, Bruno, Bruneau, Bruyer, Bruyere, Buchi, Buishier, Budd, Bunn, Burnard, Burn, Burns, Bushen, Butler, Buxton

Cadieux, Cadot, Cadotte, Cadran, Cadron, Caillancour, Caille, Caillou, Callihoo, Calder, Caldwell, Calle, Calliere, Carrier, Carriere, Chale, Cameron, Cammon, Campbell, Campeau, Campion, Canada, Caplan, Caplette, Carbier, Cardin, Cardinal, Cardinalle, Carignan, Carignant, Caron, Carouseau, Carron, Carlier, Cavelier, Cavileer, Cayen Cayenne, Ceaville, Celier, Cesliste, Chaboillez, Chaboyer, Chaboiller, Chabot, Caribou, Caribeau, Cabot, Chalifoux, Challifoux, Chalifousd, Chalifour, Chamaillard, Chamblie, Chambly, Champagne, Champagnie, Champaign, Champeau, Champoux, Champut, Chandonell, Chandonet, Chandone, Chanteloup, Chaput, Chaquet, Chaquette, Charboneau, Charet, Charette, Charleand, Charland, Charles, Charlot, Charlotte, Charon, Charron, Charpentier, Chartier, Chartrand, Chatelain, Chatellain, Chastelain, Chausse,

# Carrying the Chalice Forward

Chauvin, Chavellier, Chenail, Genail, Genaille, Chenet, Chenay, Chenet, Chenette, Cheney, Chesnay, Chenier, Chesnier, Chnier, Chernard, Chevalier, Chevallier, Chevrette, Chiron, Chouinara, Chouinard, Chouna, Chretien Chrestien, Christie, Christian, Christien, Clappen, Clark, Clarke, Clare, Cleghoin, Clemont, Clemons, Clement, Clermon, Clermond, Clermont, Cloimon, Clouseau, Clouston, Clouthier, Cloutier, ?Louttit?, Cochrane, Cockran, Colin, Collin, Colonet, Coloumbe, Comeau, Comtois, Conchois, Conner, Connolly, Constane, Constant, Contou, Contre, Contraye, Cook, Couc, Cooper, Corbett, Corbier, Corbiere, Corbeil, Courbiere, Corbin, Core, Cormier, Corner, Corrigal, Cosset, Cote, Coste, Cotte, Coton, Cotineau, Cotenoir, Cotnoir, Cotterelle, Couc, Couchois, Couin(Cowan), Coulombe, Colomb, Coulombier, Courchesne, Courchene, Coursolle, Courtel, Courtmanche, Courtemanche, Courteoreille, Courvalle, Courville, Courvillion, Couvillion, Cousineau, Coutetois, Couteau, Couture, Couturier, Couvret, Cox, Craddock, Crawford, Crebassa, Cremer, Creamer, Credit, Credy, Crequi, Crevet, Crevier, Crevillion, Crie, Crissot, Cromartie, Cromarty, Croteau, Crow, Cruson, Cummings, Cunningham, Cyr.

Dabbin, Dabin, Dahl, Dahal, Daigneau, Daigneault, Daignault, d'Alleboust, d'Allebout, Dani, Danie, Daniel, Daniels, Daoust, Daragon, D'Arpentigny, Datchy, Daunais, Dauphinais,

# Carrying the Chalice Forward

Dauphine, Daoust, David, Davies, Davis, Dayon, Daze, Dazay, de L'anglade, Deacon, Dease, DeBilly, Debin, DeCaire, Decauteau, Decoteau, Decheneau, Decoigne, Decoyne, Defaut, Defond, Defont, Degain, Degan, DeGannville, Dehi, Dehomme, Dejarlet, Dejenvier, DelaHaye, DeLaronde, Delatreille, Delisle, Deloge, Delome, Desnomme, Delaume, Delone, Delorme, Delude, Demaeru, Demarais, Desmarais, Demers, Demontigny, Demoulin, Deneau, Denege, Denig, Denis, Dennet, Dennett, Dennette, Denning, Dennis, Dennison, Denison, Denisson, Denomme, Dentte, Deolyne, Depeau, Depeaux, Depot, Deroteau, Depres, Desaintes, Desanges, Desaulniers, Desaultels, Desbiens, Deschambault, Deschamps, Descheneaux, Deschenaux, Descoleaux, De'shaw, Desilais, Desjardin, Desjardins, Desjarlais, DesLauriers, Deslisle, Desmaison, Destroismaisons, Desmarais, Desnoyer, Desnoyers, DesPortes, Desriviere, Desrosiers, Desroches, Desrochers, Detour, DeLatour, Detre, Devault, DeVos, DeVienne, Dickson, Diollette, Dionne, Dion, Divers, Divere, Divertissant, Dodge, Dogon, Doleur, Donald, Danaldson, Donnais, Doucette, Douglas, Dousman, Doyon, Dubes, Dubois, Duboishe, Duboisheu, Dubreuil, Duchaine, Duchesne, Ducharme, Duclos, Dudoiu, Dufresne, Dufond, Dufour, Duga, Dugal, Duganne, DuLigne, Dulignon, Duma, Dumas, Dumais, Dumond, Dumont, Dumonier, Dunie, Dunord, Dupis, DuPlessis,

# Carrying the Chalice Forward

DuPontbriand, Dupres, Dupre, Duperey, Dupont, Dupuis, Duquet, Duquette, Durand, Durandry, Dussault, Dusang, Dutour, Dutremble, Duval, Dyson,

Easter, Eccles, Edeline, Edinburck, Ehrler, Elemont, Elie, Emlyn, Emelin, Emeric, Emond, Emont, Eneau, Eno, Enno, Henaut, Henault, England, Erasmus, Ermatinger, Evons,

Fabien, Fafas, Fafard, Fagnand, Fagnant, Faille, Fait, Fafard, Falardeau, Falcon, Farguson, Farquharson, Faubert, Faucher, Faultenx, Favarner, Faval, Favel, Favera, Favre, Fayan, Faye, Febeau, Felion, Ferguson, Filion, Fillion, Fillon, Fera, Ferrier, Fiberault, Fichi, Fichot, Fidler, Fielding, Fiey, Filande, Filisque, Finlay, Finley, Finlayson, Finglayson, Finnegan, Firth, Fisher, Fix, Flammant, Flamand, Flett, Fleury, Folds, Folster, Fontaine, Forbes, Fornier, Forrest, Forster, Forth, Fortier, Fortur, Fortin, Fosseneuve, Fouchi, Foucille, Foufard, Foulds, Foumir, Fourer, Fournaise, Fournesse, Fournier, Fouron, Fox, Foye, Francocier, Franoeur, Francour, Francois, Franks, Fraser, Frechette, Frederick, Frederic, Frenchepan, Frenier, Freismith, Friday, Frobisher, Forbisher, Forbister, Fruchon, Fuseau

Gaboury, Gabory, Gaddy, Gadeou, Gadeau, Gager, Gagnier, Ganier, Gagnion, Gagnon, Galaneau, Galarneau, Gamelin, Gardner, Gardipuis, Gareau, Gariepy, Garrioch, Garton, Gaudry, Gaulier, Gausse, Gausselin, Gauthier,

# Carrying the Chalice Forward

Gautier, Gotier, Gauvier, Gauvin, Gendbeau, Gendren, Gendron, Genthon, George, Gepson, Gerair, Gerard, Girard, Gerardin, Gereau, Gerbeau, Gernie, Gerome, Gervais, Gesbiens, Geseron, Gibeau, Giboche, Gibson, Giguerre, Gilbert, Gill, Guill, Gillespie, Gelispie, Gillory, Gina, Gingras, Gireux, Girou, Giroux, Gladeau, Gladu, Gladue, Gladman, Glasson, God, Godd, Godin, Godon, Gonville, Gonneville, Good, Goodchild, Gordon, Goroite, Gosselin, Gouin, Goulet, Goulin, Gourneau, Goursolle, Gousson, Gesson, Grandmaison, Grandbois, Grant, Grasse, Gravalle, Graveline, Green, Gregoire, Grenier, Grenon, Grenot, Greverot, Grevote, Grey, Gray, Grignion, Grignon, Grigoire, Groat, Grondain, Grondin, Groslouis, Grouette, Groult, Groulx, Guay, Guiboche, Guilbeault, Guillon, Guillot, Guimont, Gunn, Gurneau, Gusier, Gutherie, Guthrie, Guyon

Hague, Hains, Halcro, Halcrow, Haldane, Hall, Hallett, Hamel, Hamelin, Hamilton, Hammon, Hare, Harel, Hartbridge, Harkness, Harper, Harriot, Harrison, Herrison, Harse, Harvel, Harven, Hay, Hayden, Aden, Hayes, Hayet, Haywood, Head, Hebert, Heinbrucks, Henault, Henderson, Henry, Heramai, Herbert, Herman, Heron, Herron, Herse, Heureuse, Hesse, Hibernois, Hickenberger, Higgins, Higgs, Hodgson, Hogan, Hogue, Holmes, Homand, Homan, Hoob, Hood, Hooks, Hope, Houde, Houel, Ouel, Ouelle, Houle, Hoole, Hourrie, Howard, Howse, Hubert, Hudon,

# Carrying the Chalice Forward

Hudson, Hughes, Hunt, Huppe, Hurbert, Hurteau, Hyoon

Ignace, Igrasin, Illianard, Inkster, Irbour, Irebour, Iris, Iroquois, Irvine, Isaac, Isbister

Jackson, Jacson, Jacque, Jacques, Jacquish, Jannot, Jansen, Jauvan, Jean, Jeandron, Jeannot, Jeannotte, Jeanveau, Jeanvenne, Jeanville, Jerome, Jette, Jeuffroi, Jobin, Jocealle, Johnson, Johnston, Johnstone, Jolibois, Jolicoeur, Jolie, Jones, Jordon, Joseph, Josephe, Josepht, Josephte, Jourdain, Jordan, Jourdien, Joyal, Judith, Julien, Jutras

Kamoquoy, Keith, Kenewens, Kennedy, Kerigon, Kiminitchawgan, Kimitchaw, King, Kinonchamei, Kippling, Kirkness, Klyne, Knight, Knott, Koffman, Kolliou

Labarge, LaBay, Labain, Labaie, Labe, Labelle, LeBay, Labatte, Laberge, Labine, LaBissonniere, Labombarde, Labonde, LaBonne, Labonte, Labord, Laborde, Labott, Laboucaine, Labouche, LaBruere, Lacerte, Lachaine, Lachapelle, Lachevrotiere, Lacombe, Lacompte, Laconte, Lacouture, Lacroise, Lacroix, Ladebouche, Laderoute, Ladouceur, Ladoux, Ladron, Laferte, Lafievre, Lafleur, Lafond, Lafontaine, Lafourche, Lafournaise, Laframboise, LaFrance, Lafreniere, Lafronte, Lafleur, Lagace, LaGarde, Lager, Lagenaye,

# Carrying the Chalice Forward

Lageunesse, Lagimonier, Lagumonier, Lagemonier, Lagimonier, Lasimoniere, Lejemodiere, Lagimodiere, Lagon, Lagotherie, Lahaie, LaHay, LaHaye, Lalande, Lalonde, Lalandette, Lalibert, Laliberte, Lallemand, L'Allemond, Lamadeleine, Lamarandiere, Lambert, Lamirande, Lamorandiere, Lamorandiree, Lamoine, Lamonde, Lamontagne, Lamotte, Lamourcour, Lamoureux, Lanctin, Land, Landiancour, Landre, Landrie, Landry, Lane, Laneville, Lang, Langer, Langerain, Langevin, Langevain, Langlois, Langtain, Lanivier, Lanoville, Lanschagrin, Lantier, Lapage, Lepage, LaPierre, Lapine, Laplante, Lapointe, Larain, Larance, Larence, Laurent, Larente, Laurence), Larammee, LaRamu, Laranger, Larche, L'archeveque, Lariviere, LaRocque, Larocquebrune, Laronde, DelaRonde, Larose, LaRoux, Lasatipay, Latard, Latour, Letour, Latreille, L'August, Laurain, Laurin, Lauzon, Lavalle, Lavallee, Lavallen, Laverdure, Laviolette, Lavislette, Lavoine, Lawson, Layer, Lazari, Leask, Lebeau, Lebenson, LeBlanc, LeBruere, Lebrun, Leclair, LeClaire, LeCler, LeClerc, LeComte, Lecuyer, Lecruyer, Ledoux, leDuc, Lefort, LeGable, Legault, Legaund, Legeau, Leger, Legros, Legris, Leith, Lejour, Leland, LeLoup, LeMadelaine, Lemaire, Lemay, Lemais, Lemieux, Lemeux, Lemire, Lemoine, LeMoyne, Lennier, Lennie, Lenoir, Lenoire, Leonard, l'Epaine, L'Epigne, Lepine, l'Epine, Lenoble, Lerodeur, Leramonda,

# Carrying the Chalice Forward

LeRoy, LesSard, Lesar, Lessard, lesage, Lesoir, Lesperance, l'Esperance, Lestarige, letendre, Letremble, Levard, Leveille, Levelle, Levone, Lewes, Lewis, L'hirondelle, Lillie, Lingan, Linklater, Liones, Livermois, Livingston, Livingstone, Lizotte, Local, Lodel, Logen, Logan, Loise, Lolineau, Longlin, Longtain, Loran, L'ordre, Lordu, Lorette, Lorrin, Louis, Louseman, Lousier, Lover, Loyer, Lowe, Lucier, Luciers, Lupien, Lussier, Lumarai, Lyons

MacDonald, Macdonnell, Macdougall, MacFarlane, MacGillivray, Machard, Machar, Macintosh, Mackay, Mackenzie, MacLellan, Maclennan, Macrae, Macre, Mageon, Maingains, Maingans, Maiot, Maillet, Maillot, Milo, Mainville, Major, Malaterre, Mallet, Malette, Malouin, Manseau, Manceau, Mandeville, Maranday, Marendeau, Marcelle, Marchand, Marchettant, Marcot, Marcoux, Marlot, Marion, Marly, Marois, Maron, Marougou, Marrtour, Marsand, Marsellais Marcellais, Martel, Martelle, Martia, Martin, Martineau, Maseau, Masey, Masson, Mason, Matheson, Mathew, Matlet, Matou, mattel, Maurain, Maxwell, Mayrand, McBain, McBean, McBeath, McClaren, McClillan, McCorrister, McDermot, McDonald, McDonell, McDougall, McGill, McGillis, McGillivray, McGulpin, McIntosh, McIver, McKay, McKenney, McKenzie, McLean, McLellan, McLeod, McLoughlin, McLaughlin, McMillan,

# Carrying the Chalice Forward

McMurray, McNab, McPherson, McRobb, McTavish, Mecredi, Mercredi, Meloin, Menar, Manard, Meniau, Mercier, Merlot, Merlo, Mersau, Messier, metivier, Meunier, Meyers, Michel, Miette, Migneault, Migneron, Migsanonjean, Miller, Millet, Milo, Milois, Mineville, Minnie, Minsie, Mitchell, Moar, Mode, Monbuin, Monburn, Mondin, Mondion, Monet, Monete, Monette, Monnette, Monjeunier, Monjon, Monkman, Monsigne (Monzene), Montagnais DeMontagne, Montour, Montreil, Montrel, Montreuil, Montreuille, Montriel, Montri, Moore, Moran, Morand, Morin, Moras, More, Moreau, Morelle, Morog, Morris, Morriseau (Morrisseau, Moosoo, Mousseau), Morrissette, Morrisson, Morwich, Morwick, Moses, Mouardmoust, Mozeny, Muir, Mullois, Munro, Munroe, Murray, Myott

Nabase, Nadeau, Nafretchu, Nalon, Nasseur, Nault, Neaudri, Nesketch, Neskech, Neskes, Nippissing, Nepissing, Nolin, Normin, Normand, Normandaine, Norquay, Norris, Norte, Nott, Nouvellant, Noyes

Ocher, Odin, Ojai, Ogier, Omand, Orman, Oreille, Ouellet, Ouellette, Ouillet, Ourve, Ouvie

Page, Paget, Paleman, Palladeau, Palmeau, Pambrun, Pangman, Papeur, Paquet, Pacquet, Paquette, Paquin, Pasquin, Paradis, Parent,

# Carrying the Chalice Forward

Parant, Parenteau, Parisien, Parissien, Park, Pasanne, Paschal, Patenaude, Paterson, Patrice, Patry, Patou, Paul, Payer, Payette, Pearce, Peers, Peebles, Pellan, Pellon, Pilon, Pelle, Peltier, Pelletier, Pepin, Perain, Perat, Perrault, Perrau, Perreault, Perlier, Perrigeault, Persone, Personne, Peter, Peters, Peterson, Peticlair, Petit, Petit-Clerc, Philip, Philippe, Phillips, Philp, Picard, Picotte, Piche, Pichet, Pichot, Pierogai, Pillet, Pillion, Pillon, Pilon, Pineau, Pioux, Pipique, Pitre, Pivin, Pizan, Pizanne, Plainte, Plante, Plouf, Plouffe, Blouf, Pocha, Poisson, Poissonblanc, Poitier, Poitevan, Poitras, Poitvin, Polander, Pollier, Polson, Pomert, Pominville, Ponca, Pontbriand, Porter, Portier, Portras, Potadin, Pothuin, Poulet, Poussin, Pratt, Precour, Precourt, Presot, Preveau, Prevo, Price, Primeau, Prince, Prionard, Pritchard, Proudome, Prudome, Prudomme, Proux, Prousse, Proulx, Proveau, Provo, Provost, Pruden, Ptolomee, Pullman, Puno, Purcell, Purdy, Puyotte

Quinn, Quintal, Quesnel, Quesnelle

Raboin, Racette, Raine, Range, Ranger, Ranville, Rainville, Raper, Raphael, Rapse, Rassine, Rather, Rayans, Raymond, Reaume, Rheaume, Recolet, Reed, Rel, Relle, Renaud, Rene, Repentigny, Restoul, Revol, Richard, Richards, Richardson, Richotte, Ritchot, Riear, Riel, Risineau, Risson, Rivard, Riveau, Rivel,

# Carrying the Chalice Forward

Rivet, Robert, Robertson, Robidoux, Robillard, Robinson, Robison, Robeson, Roc, Rocheblanc, Rocheblave, Rochefoucauld, Rocheleau, Rocheran, Rocque, Rocquebrune, Rodier, Roger, Roi, Roie, Roland, Rolland, Rolellert, Rollet, Rolette, Rondeau, Roques, Rori, Rose, Roze, Rosignal, Ross, Rouleau, Rousseau, Rousselle, Roussin, Roussain, Rowand, Rowland, Roy, Rushleau

Sabiston, Sabourin, Saguira, Saliot, Salle, Sale, Salois, Sallois, Salter, Samson, Sampson, Sanders, Sanderson, Sandison, Sanson, Sansoucy, Sansregret, Sarrey, Sarrere, Saucier, Saucisse, Sault, Saut, Sautie, Sceau, Saulteaux, Saunders, Sauvage, Sauve, Sauviot, Saveret, Savoyard, Sayer, Scarth, Scheidegan, Schindler, Schmidt, Scott, Sequin, Seinez, Sejourne, Senecal, Senechal, Seri, Settee, Setter, Sharon, Charon, Shaw, Short, Shults, Sichigiksa, Sire, Silveste, Sylvestre, Simon, Simoneau, Simpson, Sinclair, Siomard, Siteauleaut, Slater, Small, Smith, Solde, Soloman, Solomon, Sononaise, Sostier, Souart, Soulard, Souliere, Soutiere, Spence, Spencer, Stagnan, Stanigan, St. Amand, St. Arnaud, St. Cire, St. Clair, St. Cyr, St. Denis, St. Dennis, St. George, St. Germain, St. Jean, St. John, St. Luc, St. Mathe(St. Matte), St. Onge, St. Pierre, St. Per, St. Tomas, St. Tommas, St. Sauveur, Star??, Stead, Stevens, Stevenson, Stewart, Stone, Stranger, Stuart, Surette, Sutherland, Swain, Sylvain

# Carrying the Chalice Forward

Tabeau, Tibeau, Taffer, Taillefer, Taitt, Tait, Tanner, Tate, Tatreau, Taurel, Tavarnier, Taylor, Tellier, Teneau, Tessier, Tetreault, Tifault, Thifault, Thiffault, Thyfault, Theret, Therese, Theroux, Therrien, Thibault, Thibert, Thomas, Thompson, Thome, Thorn, Tiche, Tiebowajam, Tiennote, Tission, Tizainne, Todd, Tomereau, Totrain, Tourangeau, Touron, Tourand, Tourond, Tourville, Tremble, Trottier, Trudomme, Truthwaite, Tuppeir, Turcotte, Turel, Turelle, Turgeon, Traill, Tulloch, Turner, Turpin, Turssin, Twat

Urtubise

Vaillancourt, Vaillencourt, Vaillancour, Valade, Valeur, Valiquette, Vallee, Valler, Valleneuve, Vanase, Vanas, Vannart, Vandreil, Vandal, Vandalle, Varin, Vary, Varry, Vassear, Vasseur, Vaudri, Vaudry, Veaudre, Vendette, Vandet, Venne, Vermette, Veronique, Versailles, Villebrun, Villebrune, Villeneuve, Villenouve, Villiers, Vincent, Vivier, Vaudry, Voudrie, Vol, Vole, Voller, Voydi

Wabikiniu, Waketch, Ward, Warring, Wassaloski, Waters, Waweh, Welch, Welsh, Wells, Wensell, White, Whitehead, Whitford, Whitway, Whiteway, Wilkie, Willette, Williams, Williamson, Ouilliamson, Wills, Wilmet, Wilmot, Wilson, Wimette, Wintzel, Wishart, Wood, Woods, Work

# Carrying the Chalice Forward

Xuisson

Yarns, Yeoph, Yopch, Yoph, Young

Zastre, Zace.

# Carrying the Chalice Forward

**The Calias Flag**

Carrying the Chalice Forward

# 11

# *Feudal Rule in the Americas*

Carrying the Chalice Forward

# 11

## *A Short History of Feudal Rule in the Americas*

**M**any may wonder where our existing form of governance within the boundaries of Canada actually came from. Others may just deftly be asleep and not mind paying 60% of their income in taxes. On the other hand, if any thought is given to the origin of the colonial ideal, then maybe a look at our feudal origins will help.

The early governance models for Canada were modeled on what the early papacy had helped initiate throughout Italy in the 12$^{th}$ century in order to gain control of the indigenous economies and revenue flows of the populations; oh yes, and the land and people too.

According to the Encyclopedia Britannica first edition, 1771: Legislated "...heritable rights are governed by the feudal law, which owed its origin, or at least its first improvements, to the Longobards; whose kings, upon having penetrated into Italy, the better to preserve their conquests, made grants to their principal

## Carrying the Chalice Forward

commanders of great part of the conquered provinces, to be again sub-divided by them amoung the lower officers, under the conditions of fidelity and military service."

"The feudal constitutions and usages were first reduced into writing, about the year 1150, by two lawyers of Milan, under the title Consuetudines Feudorum. ...It is generally agreed, that it had the tacit approbation, and was considered as the customary feudal law of all the countries subject to the empire. ...He who makes the grant is called the superior, and he who receives it the vassal."

When, at the start of the seventeenth century, the French Crown introduced their version of feudal law for the Americas they didn't quite sit down and explain the dualist philosophy of the papist authorities, who also held power over the souls of the French and anyone with whom they wanted to be allies. When the indigenous families agreed to the alliance terms with the French "to live together as one family" they could not fully comprehend that their new Jesuit uncles could also force their rule of authority over them as well. This dichotomy of the body and soul was inconceivable to the traditional rule and indigenous understanding of law.

# Carrying the Chalice Forward

The changeable rules of the feudal system allowed an indigenous person to still be indigenous yet gain access to the rights of a French citizen through receiving protection in the forts, at times of attack; and the rights to own lands and improvements without being infringed upon by other French settlers or other foreigners. What wasn't discussed, or fully made plain, was how the French citizens had to surrender to the superiority of the Vatican in regard to their souls. So what seems simple from a family perspective of who gets to be protected changes to: only the baptized get to be protected. This seesaw approach of who had power over the souls of the indigenous people became quite confusing, even at the best of times.

Many of the freeborn French stood against these rules and provided the real protection for the indigenous families by joining their bloodlines together as permanent allies. The so-called laissez-faire approach of these early families to this situation was to unilaterally become godparents to their allied indigenous families, and adopt their children; so that if anything happened to the parents the children would just be regarded as the children of the god-parents; automatically becoming full French citizens. In this way, many of the genealogies modern families rely on to show their French heritage when compared to DNA trails find themselves becoming more and more indigenous.

# Carrying the Chalice Forward

After the Jesuits had managed to build up enough land and financial holdings, they were strong enough that by around 1670, they forced the demand that only Christian (baptized) peoples could gain entrance to the forts during times of crisis. This edict did not sit well with the allied chiefs and leaders of the families, yet it showed each of them the inhumane duplicity of the priests and made plain their agendas of forcing the capitulation of beliefs. By gaining control of the physical life and of the spiritual life, including the afterlife, the tag-team of the French colonials and the religious neophytes was able to almost demolish the foundations of indigenous life and liberty. Even our Valois cousins who chose to join us at this time were required to undergo abjurations to absolve themselves of their heretical nature in order to even enter the territories. The Vatican almost won its feudal campaign for control over the spirit of the indigenous soul, yet did not count on our family's stepping in to help change things.

It is good to remember that the English and their allies at this time coveted the land of the Huron and staged many incidents; in conjunction with the help of the Jesuits and other priests, to take possession of the lands. Eventually the peace hoped for by our ancestors was denied and ensuing war and

# Carrying the Chalice Forward

death brought the country to a point of desolation and pain. Many of the families felt the betrayals of these political demands, yet held to the true peace that was founded in the visions of their ancient grandfathers.

In the heat of these battles for the indigenous souls and the soul of the Americas, the Jerusalem families underwrote the construction of hospitals in Quebec and Montreal. The Hospitaliers, under the adept guidance of Jeanne Mance and the master architect mason, Charles D'Alleboust; funded by the Godfrey de Bouillion pledge, managed to keep peace and secure the true familial alliance hoped for by our united ancestors. These hands-on efforts for peace provided a strengthening of the blood bonds between all of our families. By 1701 the papacy had lost great ground by the up-swelling of the bonds of allegiance between our Huron, Algonquin and other indigenous families, including the early Bois Brule lines. Our true defense against the pernicious aggression of the bureaucracy has always been to bide the time and stay true to the hearts of the people by first being and remaining a family. In this case we became a very large indigenous family.

The Great Peace of 1701 bears witness to the almost total tribal mixing of up to 100 indigenous tribes of nations, with each other;

## Carrying the Chalice Forward

and with the early Norman French speaking families. Following the wars, challenges, exoduses and expulsions of the previous century, the bloodlines and histories of most main families became joined with the free roaming Bois Brule. It seems these bloodlines held a greater resilience against the foreign diseases and other intrigues. With our families and cultures merging continually over the next hundred years we forged strong roots until the English managed to gain an advantage over the Colonial French and claimed feudal title control over the Americas.

At the time when the English assumed control of the territories they were still more in line with the racist ideals of the papacy and had not yet managed to overcome their reticence to joining their families fully or equally with the indigenous peoples. Some English and Dutch families had embraced the true peace with the families and had merged their lineages, yet this was not the norm. The French and Scottish models of alliance prior to the English fit very well with the indigenous traditions of marrying outside of their clans and nations. The change following the defeat of the French to the English, initiating the change from French feudal law to English feudal law, showed the unconscionable versatility and ultimate brutality capable with the feudal system when combined with unbridled power. This time may be called: "the time of the great

## Carrying the Chalice Forward

reversal" for our families.

Following the British tea party war with the States, the lands of Upper and Lower Canada were divided into feudal holdings for the military and UEL loyalists. By 1800 and the conversion of the colony to English based terms of occupation and law, the French and the indigenous families found themselves at an extreme disadvantage. The terms of English feudal occupation of the land meant the elimination of French merchant licenses and often their rights to free title and use of their previously held properties. The Scottish, some English and some Irish-born merchants, united with the old French and Bois Brule/Metis families and obtained the necessary trade licenses to continue the indigenous, allied merchant economy. This merger of these families actually provided the backbone for the true spirit and perseverance for what is known as the true spirit of the land (L'esprit du nord). The inhumanity and the losses to the families from the bottom of Florida on up, by the full change to the rule of English law, brought many families to a state of destitution, and yet steeled their determination to survive, with help from their old allies.

The feudal subdivision of the land happened again after 1812, except that the Bois Brule families who had helped to defend Canada

# Carrying the Chalice Forward

from invasion by the States somehow managed to lose the remaining parts of their lands out west, as well as their trading economies south of the border. This does not even touch on the great inequity of being passed over for loyalty grants given primarily to English speaking mercenaries. This style of perfidy by the English wore on just like an individual vendetta from the top to the bottom of their hierarchy. Our families did eventually manage to sell their southern trading posts to J. J. Astor, yet ended up losing many additional settlements to the points of a compass. The Indian Department and the military decided it was best to have the Bois Brule/Metis keep moving from their properties to allow space for the new settlers. All in all some not very nice things happened over the unending greed for control of the land.

The Bois Brule watched as their French and Scottish protected titles to the land disappeared; whereby under English law they were considered to be 100% indigenous and not allowed to inherit title to properties. Many court battles were fought with little reward or advantage; at least not until most of the properties were appropriated by others. The Bois Brule shook the English world by defending their inherent right to their territories by standing against the racist attacks and removing the unwelcome settlers at the White Oaks Crossing around 1817. After our

# Carrying the Chalice Forward

NWC partners lost control of the allied indigenous economy, and way of life, through the forced merger with the English Crown-sponsored HBC, and the timely sale by Napoleon of our free territorial lands in the US, we became hedged in between a rock and a hard place. Many of our families kept moving further west or became American, or British, or feudally-controlled French, or stayed under the Indian act. It seemed for most that our hopes were in vain for the avoiding of the loss of our settlement lands or connections to our old families and our family's territories.

A few decades later, when the time came to hand over the control of the feudal-held territory of upper and lower Canada to the new Canadians the idea of the feudal flow of funds held great interest to the bureaucrats of the time. What better way to run the country than to have every one paying for it with the sweat from their brows. By 1870 when the new Canadians followed the feudal approach of the English and showed up across the west to annex the rest of our families' holdings, we put our foot down, and formed the province of Manitoba, to defend our inherent Bois Brule/Metis title. This still didn't stop them from taking the land, as they controlled the law to the point of making it legal for 3 year old Bois Brule/Metis children to sell their titles to the priests and other speculators.

# Carrying the Chalice Forward

By 1885 the new Canadians had united in the plan to prompt our families to take up arms; and with the help of the church and others as spies and instigators, made their plans to evict us. These moves were not supported by many of our old families, who were still the peacekeepers; and who knew well the losses that would happen from this charade. The completion of the plan of the English proto-feudal system seemed to be to have all Bois Brule and other indigenous families surrender their existing settlements, with improvements, to the newcomers; have us all move to deserted areas where food and shelter was scarce, or move to overcrowded areas with other families; and finally to tire of being free and surrender our indigenous titles and rights and just pay taxes, yet without the same or equal benefits of the other citizens. This became a take-it-or-leave-it offer during most of the short discussions and meetings. If we didn't move they would prompt us into armed conflict and then take the land by force. We didn't move so they chose their preference for using brute force.

These same agendas seem to be still carried on today, with many nations surrendering their indigenous rights for full tax paying ownership of the land; and by the implementing of new taxation systems on the reserves. The variety of

# Carrying the Chalice Forward

life the indigenous world offers the rest of creation is well worth taking some time to reconsider its total destruction. If we look at the destruction to the rest of the lands in the old world, and the continued expansion of the deserts; and look at the ongoing industrial abuses and damage caused by the neglect of the natural world, some sanity should soon hopefully prevail. Our understanding is that only through uniting with the indigenous world can any people or nation ever hope to retain any form of inheritance for their children and their descendants. We must now all be adults and deal fairly with the land, and its peoples; and allow the real dreams of our ancient elders to inspire us with the inherent freedom to exist and prosper together as equals.

The main dilemma of this modern proto-feudal economic system is that it is not rooted in the indigenous heart of caring for the land, and the four-footed animals; and other living expressions of the rest of creation. Our belief is that: as the families awake from their sleep of oppression, and see the destruction this lack of conscience provides; they will join together in alliance with the earth, and with the other families, to arise and remain free of this mindless destruction of the planet. Our cousins in Italy, Spain, Portugal, France, Ireland, Scotland, England, Denmark and elsewhere will hopefully re-join hands with nature, and

# Carrying the Chalice Forward

with our families: to help preserve life and freedom for the true descendants of peace.

By fulfilling the vision of a healed land filled with loving, happy and beautiful people, the full attainment of Peace is our only real option. This may only be accomplished by all families sitting at the same table and equally surrendering the claims and pains of the past; and starting over with the indigenous families, from whatever part of the world they originate from, each fully and equally included.

Carrying the Chalice Forward

# *Biographical Sketch of the Author*

I was born in Vancouver in 1957. A traumatic birth where the doctors, after keeping me in an incubator the size of a car for a month or so, handed me back to my mom and said "we almost lost him." That's the closest they got to admitting something might have happened. I grew up in Manitoba and Alberta, coming to Ontario in 1987. My son, Benjamin, was born in 1997 and lives with me still. Whether as a result of my birth journey, or some other event, I have felt and known a direct connection to all of my ancestors and have spent my physical life reconnecting the dots. Spending time in a library or reading old books is an everyday enjoyable and entrancing part of my life still.

My own passion for writing and research has flourished throughout my life and is reflected in my own experiences and studies. While attending university majoring in English and Philosophy I realized that I needed to experience life first, to be able to add any strength to the telling of a true story. My research delved quite deeply into the origins of our families, and of how we managed to get ourselves boxed into so many corners. What I have discerned is that when you hold a bright

# Carrying the Chalice Forward

light a lot of things show up that you may not necessarily enjoy.

My desire now is to place some of the memories and stories into print so they will be readily available for others.

The truth of our understanding of family is that we are the sum of the parts of our ancestors we wish to be known for; and the sum of some of our ancestors we wish history had forgotten to tell us about. The unifying theme of most of my research has revolved around the origins and depth of the Bois Brule/ Metis lineages. Since hearing the violin as a baby and being surrounded by family at gatherings and events, the web which holds us together as a family has always fascinated me. The story of my own life is as a reflection of our combined Bois Brule/Metis story, as we each hold part of the purpose for getting to know the truth - as much as that is possible in the world today. We cannot tell a Bois Brule/Metis story without first telling the stories about whom and what we are.

The Bois Brule/Metis, due to our own challenges, did not write many of the histories so far published about our families. We are Bois Brule/Metis descended from many known figures in the general history of the Americas. We descend from the majority of the furtrade families including the original nobles

## Carrying the Chalice Forward

and habitants of New France and Acadia. These main lines provide the genetic makeup for many of our main Bois Brule/Metis original families.

Since 1978 we have researched our own family's history and genealogy with thousands of direct ancestors back through the 1500's and 1600's. Surprisingly, many of these were from previous alliances and connections through to the start of the Middle Ages and prior. Some of the families we directly descend from are an important part of the research because they include what are sometimes referred to as the Lorraine families. Others include the Stuart, Clan Chattan, Jacobite, Fenian, Ui Neill, Ard Ri, and other allied families and the histories including many of those of grail/Masonic lore. Our indigenous lines connect with many families already written of in many history books, although our version of the tale may be somewhat different.

A story about the Bois Brule/Metis seems more real when some of the pivotal figures of importance are known. The following are a short list of some of the important figures in our own family's story.

Susan: Swampy Cree from Pinehouse Lake Saskatchewan, wife of William MacGillivray, head of the NWC company, and the mother of twins Simon Jnr. and Joseph MacGillivray.

# Carrying the Chalice Forward

Susan's marriage helped strengthen the trade enough for William to become the head of the NWC. She was a sash-maker and an artisan.

William MacGillivray: Head of the NWC, Grand Master for the Masonic Lodge of Lower Canada, MLA, Lieutenant Colonel under General McGill in the Army defending Canada against the American invasion of 1812, CEO of the Lower Canada Land Development Corporation. During the impending forced merger in 1821 with the HBC, the native chiefs gathered in Montreal and awarded William the permanent title forever of "Great White Father" to honour the loving relationships he held with our indigenous families.

Prior to his death in 1825, our family's St. Regis lands (*originally designated as inheritance for his two Bois Brule/Metis sons: Simon and Joseph*) were exchanged with the Crown, at the personal request of King George; for a promise of 6,000 acres in the Ottawa valley valued at over $100,000 English pounds (in 1810 currency). Eventually less valuable lands in a different area were patented to William. In his will, these 6,000 acres were designated as the sole inheritance for his twin Bois Brule/Metis sons. After 20 years of court battles successfully proving the right of lawful inheritance, these lands were never transferred by the crown. Similar instances happened to almost every mixed blood child listed in the

# Carrying the Chalice Forward

wills of their non-indigenous parents. Our family still holds title claims to over 125,000 acres of prime city lands, as well as other tracts and parcels, for which the crown tacitly remains silent.

In another 20 years, by 1846, the agendas were switched so that Bois Brule/ Metis descendants were not allowed to claim their indigenous rights; and were assaulted and chased off their family's settlements, without being provided any form of compensation. We became the knot in the middle of the legislative tug of war. Depending on which box they wanted to put us in was dependant only on how bad they wanted the land. Eventually they decided that a pine box was best and set their agendas accordingly. By 1869 they sent the surveyors to measure the size of the box they needed; and in 1885 they sent the Gatling crew to hammer us into the box, yet all they killed was a 12 year old innocent boy. One can see why our family originally forbade the entry of lawyers into our territories.

Therese Roy: daughter of Vincent Roy Snr. and Kenewens, married to Simon MacGillivray Jnr. She was a well loved matriarch whose renowned skill as a sash-maker, quill worker and moccasin maker followed her in her journeys all across this country.

# Carrying the Chalice Forward

Kenewens: from a traditional Chippewa head family that provided massive financial and territorial benefit to most of the Chippewa family trading alliances based out of Michigan, she was married to Vincent Roy Snr.

Solomon Hamelin: (named Yellow Hair by the Lakota). The patriarch and founding main family of the Bois Brule buffalo hunting bands on the Great Plains and MLA for Manitoba, and Metis representative for the previous provisional territorial council for Rupert's land. Was often asked by many different nations to intercede and help negotiate settlements for peace between neighbouring bands on the Great Plains.

Josephte Hamelin: youngest daughter of Solomon Hamelin, supposedly originally engaged to Louis David Riel but a rift happened in the relationship and the family later disapproved of him. Josephte married Jean Baptiste Plouffe whose family originally owned Ile d'Jesus just west of Montreal. The Plouffe family was instrumental in providing financial and logistical support for our families in the defense of our freedom and our territories in the Northwest.

Joseph MacDougall: (last remaining fur buyer in the 1930's when they closed the old fort in Red River). The family owned a large portion of the original St. Vital parish lands referred to

## Carrying the Chalice Forward

as "our homeland" in Fort Garry Manitoba, son of Duncan MacDougall. When Riel was being transported, Duncan tried to stop the hanging party from crossing the river and only agreed to let them pass after looking down the barrel of a gun himself. (of the Clairvous lineage).

Jean Celier (Carriere): whose family originally arrived with Jeanne Manse aboard the Andre in 1659 to help with the founding of Mount Royal. While working on the building of the Hospital for Quebec, Jean met with Barbe Halle and became engaged and, according to noble traditions, married through signing a marriage treaty. This family is connected to the Clare, Cari and Caille lineage of antiquity.

Marie Boucher: the Bois Brule 12-year-old wife of Governor Pierre Boucher: the founder of Boucherville, who brought together many of our families around a central push to go further west.

Joseph Saguirou Gauthier: (LaVerendrye's full-blooded Algonquin great uncle). He and his brother, Jean Baptiste Gauthier, were both licensed as French merchants before 1690. Joseph Saguirou and Jeanne Maxoumi-timousens were their full-blooded Algonquin parents. Following the death of their parents fighting the Iroquois their Gauthier god-parents baptized them as their own children.

# Carrying the Chalice Forward

Euphrosine Magdeleine Nicolet: the Bois Brule daughter of Jeanne Bahmahmaadjimiwin of Nipissing origin and Chief Jean Nicolet the explorer.

Jean Baptiste Perrault: who brought our early family of nations together for peace and alliance.

Catherine Anenontak: the daughter of Chief Nicolas Arendakohi and Marie Outriouendat (Of the Cord and Wendat families) married to Jean Durand and was Matriarch to a trade empire known primarily as the Lafleur era.

Cree woman: married to Laurent Cadotte, Laurent's sons were chiefs for the Chippewa trading settlements of Sault Ste. Marie and Thunderbay.

Charlotte Marougou: Cree woman married to Thomas Edeline (Dion)

Woman of the Peace River Band: married to Paul St. Germain.

Marie Caribou: daughter of Joseph Chabot and Madeleine Coulombe. At the combining of the Chabot and the Coulombe lineages the Chabot name for some reason was changed to Caribou. At that time period there was a lot of persecution of our families and it may have

## Carrying the Chalice Forward

just been easier to change it than deal with the threats of persecution by the English because of fears of the potential inherent right to claim English title to their territories as rightful descendants of the Cabot lineage and the 1497 charter.

Angelique Saulteaux: married to Antoine Vandale, a very old family.

Marie Miteouamegoukoue: married to Pierre Couc, son of Nicolas Couc and Elizabeth Templair, uniting our Iroquoian Bois Brule traditions with the Mohawk lineages has sprouted descendants from one coast to the other.

...and many, many more...

Many of the lines we descend from are from old Acadian and Norman lines. We still continue to help many innumerable families reconnect with their relatives and their past. One of the questions we use to guide our searches is to find out why the English are so afraid of us? We have continually approached the research with a desire to understand this simple question to help explain why, on so many occasions; we were persecuted so strongly by the governments, crowns and churches? After robbing our families of most of our lands and holdings, the agents for the churches and the crown continued with their

## Carrying the Chalice Forward

agendas of segregation and molestation to wear us down, and berate us, hoping we would forget what the fight was about. As the seed of Abraham, we could never forget that the fight is only ever about freedom; and with the knowledge that we are the creator's allies and were brought to our territories for great and beautiful purpose, all we need do is breath for the English to tremble at our sight.

Our search has also been to really determine "What is the threat of the continued existence and prosperity of the Metis?" The answers we have so far received are continually supported and expanded by other family members and lines, almost like the ongoing story of David and Goliath - except in technicolour.

When the members of the Sinclair family expressed their desire, and showed their great intent, to rebind the lines of our families; our combined research stretched further to include many of our older families and histories. The research has taken on a new energy and completion in knowing our extended family's desire to bring us all back together.

For most of my adult life, I have belonged to and helped many different Native community organizations and been active in the indigenous Métis community. I hold great enjoyment being involved with the various advisory councils and other historic Metis

# Carrying the Chalice Forward

Community groups. In a casual way I very much enjoy the story part of meeting and talking with cousins from every walk of life. My greatest joy is dancing in regalia or to the violin. Spending time talking with our elders and storytellers has brought a refined gentleness to the understandings we have of ourselves and each other. My main love, as I see it, though, is keeping our families on track and helping our children remember who we really are and what are our true stories.

A general theme within many of our families, at this point, is that it is very important for some of us to step forward and help inform the rest of our younger families of our true origins. In this way we hope to enlighten and entertain their minds and hearts with our own understandings of things. We may not all agree as to the reasons for all the things that have befallen us, but we can still enjoy the learning and renewal of being together.

"Our family and our heritage are surrounded by miracles and our true foundations include the rocks, the sun, the clouds, the sky, the water and the soil. We are still a tall tower of hope for all people who desire to be free."

Our writing and our telling of stories is part of the elegance of who we are as a people. We can often look a bit daunting and rough and yet speak with the voices of angels. Being of

# Carrying the Chalice Forward

Viking, Irish and Indigenous origins, many of our people cover a full range of body types, from tiny to grand. We tend to be quite handsome — or so we've been led to believe; and well-built, too. So when, innocently, a 6'8", 300 lb. man walks up to the podium and reads a sonnet praising the intricate frosty designs on his window courtesy of a visit from Jack Frost the night before; and then apologizes after he snaps a six foot beam in two when he forgot to duck under a door frame; you are left to wonder at how the Jesuits were ever foolish enough to attempt to try to tell us what to do.

It is my desire to write elegantly, yet in my innocence I may bring forth some crude comments and ideas. Should I offend anyone, I am now taking the time to beg your forgiveness, hoping that we may, once again, all laugh together. For those already laughing, it is my wish to illuminate the illusion that continues to exist, deshrouding the innocence yet further from the guilt we sometimes wear like a warm blanket.

Truth be told, though, in this world we are neither innocent nor guilty; we are simply the Creator's means of deriving humour from our challenges.

The heart of what I have meditated on for several decades now is "How do we create a peaceful worldwide community?" Most people

## Carrying the Chalice Forward

have a tendency to leave things to the last minute. I, too, must confess my humanity and my tardiness in waiting so long. We seem to like to wait until someone else does something noteworthy first. However, waiting until all the different peoples of the world are raising up weapons of war against each other is like waiting until the forest fire reaches the edge of your house before you throw your bucket of water on it. The answer to our worldwide shared dilemma is that in receiving our own wake-up call we must then act on our visions of a healed world, through embracing the peace of the world with all of our soul and heart. In this way, we are creating a conscious action in keeping with our decisions to live the higher traditions of peace, caring and sharing. By turning our reliance from using weapons of war into responding with loving and nurturing support for all life we become truly free.

Could it be just that we need this pressure to get past our being just a bunch of lazy teenagers dolled into sleep? Perhaps in desiring peace for the world the real questions we can then ask are: "How are we going to use our own buckets to save the world?" When faced with the reality of our own burning house we must each answer the question "What are we going to put in our buckets -- water or gas?"

# Carrying the Chalice Forward

What is it that each of us strives for on this earth? What is it that we can come to equal terms on? Do we all want to be lords, ladies, masters and conquerors? Would we each enjoy being gardeners, maids and carpenters? At some point, we each have to make an important decision by actually asking ourselves what it is that other people want, as well as the more deeply philosophical questions of "Why are we each here on this earth? What does the Creator have in store for each of us? What do we each have in store for creation? How do we conduct our lives so as to be a benefit to creation? How do we go beyond just being an element of destruction? What does each of us have to agree to so that we can live together in peace?"

Defending our rights to live in peace is an ongoing question within the systems of governance today. How do we protect our inherent rights to: Be on the earth? Live where we choose? Live according to whatever our traditions support? Get what we want? Live with each other on the earth in peace? How can we do this: without surrendering who we are, and without severing ourselves from our own traditions? How can we all achieve living in peaceful co-existence, together with all of humanity?

Many religions and governments say they have these solutions. Yet, through their inquisitive

## Carrying the Chalice Forward

examples, they have already shown their inability to accomplish any form of lasting peace. Whether it is, by the very nature of their bureaucracies, that neither can give honour to any form of life in the natural world; or that the ability to share is not in their skill set. Does any of this matter? Is it too late for the balance of the natural world to bounce back? Is there time to still be able to help nurture an ecosystem capable of supporting human life, animal life, plant life and industrial life for the future?

It is our fervent belief that if we agree to live together in peace and harmony with the earth, the rest will surely follow. While attending the first open Chief's conference (the first time in 125 years that the hereditary chiefs were allowed to meet in public), in Edmonton in 1990; from the first beat of the elder's drum I was on a spirit journey. The story I wrote and placed on my cousin's, Chief Dion of Enoch, plate at the banquet told the story of how the meetings and discussions would go that day. The understanding of what took place as it matched the story startled my cousin and impacted the event in his memory. When the hereditary chiefs finally stood up near the end to lead the remainder of the chiefs in pledging to help the earth against the destruction of her waters and sacred places they were supported by the majority of the families present.

# Carrying the Chalice Forward

All of our old families (at one time or another) have drawn swords against each other. In the same way, we have all agreed to allow harm and destruction to come to different parts of the earth and the natural ecosystems. The only abiding solution we can see to reversing this destruction is to surrender to peace through rebuilding our relationships with the help of creation. Worldwide peace will help heal the imbalance of the earth. Worldwide peace will stop the continued destruction. Earth-based, environmentally conscious, governance models can work to restore the healthy natural balance of life. There really is only this one solution. Through forgiving and healing each part of creation, (including each other) we will begin to build a future rich with health and benefit for the earth and all of our future descendants and dependants.

Through understanding and keeping the teachings of the Great laws of peace and being tender with one another we can surrender to the inherent beauty and majesty of Mother Earth and bring peace to the worldwide humanity.

# Carrying the Chalice Forward